Inside the Flower Garland Sutra

Huayan Buddhism and the Modern World

Ben Connelly

With translations by Weijen Teng

Foreword by Ruben L. F. Habito

Wisdom Publications
132 Perry Street
New York, NY 10014 USA
wisdom.org

Library of Congress Cataloging-in-Publication Data
Names: Connelly, Ben, author.
Title: Inside the Flower Garland Sutra: Huayan Buddhism and the modern world / Ben Connelly.
Description: New York, NY, USA: Wisdom, [2024] | Includes bibliographical references and index.
Identifiers: LCCN 2024042823 (print) | LCCN 2024042824 (ebook) | ISBN 9781614298779 (paperback) | ISBN 9781614298854 (ebook)
Subjects: LCSH: Hua yan Buddhism—Doctrines. | Buddhist philosophy. | Buddhism—Social aspects.
Classification: LCC BQ8218.3 .C66 2024 (print) | LCC BQ8218.3 (ebook) | DDC 181/.043—dc23/eng/20250111
LC record available at https://lccn.loc.gov/2024042823
LC ebook record available at https://lccn.loc.gov/2024042824

ISBN 978-1-61429-877-9 ebook ISBN 978-1-61429-885-4

29 28 27 26 25 5 4 3 2 1

Cover design by Marc Whitaker. Interior design by Gopa & Ted 2. Typeset by James D. Skatges.

Cover image: Buddhist Sutra: Hwaŏm Kyŏng (Chinese, Huayan Jing; Sanskrit, Avatamsaka Sutra), Chapter 77, with Frontispiece, early 15th century. Harvard Art Museums/Arthur M. Sackler Museum, Gift of Philip Hofer.

Printed on acid-free paper that meets the guidelines for permanence and durability of the Production Guidelines for Book Longevity of the Council on Library Resources.

Printed in the United States of America.

FSC www.fsc.org MIX Paper | Supporting responsible forestry FSC® C005010

Please visit fscus.org.

Advance Praise for
Inside the Flower Garland Sutra

"Ben Connelly's contemporary commentary on thirty verses of a Huayan classic brings the profundity of an ancient tradition right into the palm of our hands. It skillfully evokes awe with the interconnectedness of everything in magical display, illuminating this very moment."
—Judith Simmer-Brown, Naropa University, and author of *Dakini's Warm Breath: The Feminine Principle in Tibetan Buddhism*

"Ben Connelly's writing goes straight to my heart and strengthens my spirit. In this jewel of a book, he does what he knows how to do so well—he shows me that my own twenty-first-century life and a seventh-century Buddhist text can talk to each other. Whether you are a scholar of Buddhism or someone who has just begun to meditate, this book will encourage you."
—Susan Moon, co-editor of *The Hidden Lamp: Stories from Twenty-Five Centuries of Awakened Women*

"Ben Connelly's new book, *Inside the Flower Garland Sutra*, is a significant landmark in the development of Western Buddhist practice. Huayan Buddhism arose in China inspired by the massive, psychedelic *Avatamsaka Sutra—Huayan* in Chinese, *Hwaeom* in Korean, *Kegon* in Japanese, and *Flower Ornament* in English. In his previous books such as *Vasubandhu's Three Natures: A Practitioner's Guide for Liberation* and *Inside the Grass Hut: Living Shitou's Classic Zen Poem*, Connelly used primary texts to open up practical implications and expressions. Similarly, this book comments on a stimulating thirty-line verse, 'Seal of the Huayan One Vehicle Dharma Realm' by the seventh-century monk Uisang, a founder of Korean Hwaeom Buddhism, as Huayan teachings became most influential in Korea. Huayan and its key Fourfold Dharmadhatu teaching was also a pivotal inspiration for Chinese Soto Zen (or Caodong) and its Five Positions dialectical teaching. Connelly skillfully explicates this intricate Fourfold Dharmadhatu, celebrating 'the boundless harmony and joy that comes from seeing that everything is included in each thing.' Huayan is not only foundational for Hwaeom and Soto Zen, but is deeply embedded in all schools of East Asian Buddhism, as verified in a recent academic conference.

"Connelly has done his homework, consulting Korean Buddhist scholars and practitioners among others. While clarifying major Huayan teachings, he adds illuminating personal reflections based on his own years of practice and Dharma study. For example, commenting on a line about the peacefulness of all phenomena, Connelly recounts the moment when he awakened from pride in his own addiction, and the peacefulness of meditators joining a gathering in his Minneapolis neighborhood to celebrate the verdicts after the trial for the George Floyd murderers. Commenting on the Huayan ancestor Fazang's mirrored hall demonstrating to Empress Wu the radical interconnectedness of all things, Connelly applies this to time: 'All of time only and always shows up in the form of particular moments . . . Moments don't have boundaries.' Connelly then cites James Baldwin, including 'History is literally present in all we do,' and Dogen on time flowing, 'Without your complete effort right now, nothing would be actualized.' Describing the tumult after the George Floyd murder, and his own efforts to express the wholeness of the Ocean Mirror Mind, Connelly mentions Marvin Gaye, Aretha Franklin, Kendrick Lamar, and the American Indian Movement. Connelly further recommends Uisang's verse as a *dharani*, helpful to simply chant without concern about itemizing meanings. Uisang's song culminates with the original stillness that is Buddha. Connelly here speaks of the value of joyfulness, replete in the *Huayan Sutra*. 'Our lives matter, suffering matters, and our practice matters. Each of us has the opportunity, a precious jewel, to find our way.' I am deeply grateful to Ben Connelly for this excellent book, so supportive as we face a time of challenge."

—Taigen Dan Leighton, author of books of Buddhist commentary and translation including *Just This Is It: Dongshan and the Practice of Suchness*, *Faces of Compassion: Classic Bodhisattva Archetypes*, and *Dogen's Extensive Record*

"This jewel-like book is very much a Zen teacher and lifelong practitioner's journal, consisting of brief chapters of warm-hearted reflections on various phrases (in translation) from the *Avatamsaka Sutra* and Korean master Uisang's Ocean Seal diagram. Each chapter reflects the author's curiosity, delight, and unfolding personal spiritual insights that arise as he immerses himself in the dazzling abundance of Huayan Buddhism."
—Mushim Patricia Ikeda, Buddhist teacher and community activist

Contents

Foreword

Infinity Right Here Now: A Journey of Coming Home

> To see a world in a grain of sand
> And a heaven in a wild flower
> Hold infinity in the palm of your hand
> And eternity in an hour
> —William Blake, "Auguries of Innocence"

The poet William Blake must have had a glimpse of that world that is portrayed with much elaborate language in the *Avatamsaka*, or *Flower Garland, Sutra*, a Buddhist scriptural text dating back to the early centuries of the Common Era composed in India and transmitted later to neighboring Asian countries. This sutra is a rather voluminous collection of scriptural texts which became the basis for a school of thought and practice in East Asia known as Huayan (Hwaeom in Korean, Kegon in Japanese) Buddhism, which in time came to influence other schools, most notably the Chan (Seon in Korean, Zen in Japanese) Buddhist tradition.

This sutra, as with every other sutra in the Buddhist canon, is meant to convey what the Buddha realized and taught to his followers. A section of the sutra tells the story of the pilgrim Sudhana, who undertakes a journey in search of truth, and who visits with and learns from fifty-three enlightened teachers and gurus who had reputedly also seen what the Buddha saw.

Huayan philosophers Dushun (557–640), Fazang (643–712), and others have waxed profound on this world of enlightenment experienced by the Buddha in their own treatises commenting on the *Flower Garland Sutra*. They highlight the image of the Net of Indra, a vast and infinite web of jewels wherein each jewel contains and reflects in itself the entirety of all jewels, and vice versa, wherein all jewels contain and reflect every single jewel in the entire net. The message is, in short, that each one thing that exists in this universe, likened to a jewel—you, me, dogs, cats, trees, clouds, mountains, rivers, the sun, the moon, every star, every blade of grass, every speck of dust—contains and reflects each and everything else within itself. Everything is complete in itself, as it contains the whole, and there is nothing in this universe that is not contained and held in all the other things in the universe.

This is a breathtaking vision of a wondrous world that ultimately defies verbal and conceptual articulation, which many mystics and poets across the ages and across religious traditions or no religious tradition have been speaking or writing about in their various ways. It was the entry into this world that transformed the life of one Siddhartha Gautama, a prince-turned-mendicant-seeker grappling with this dissatisfactory human condition and seeking liberation, in an experience that came to him as he sat in silent meditation under a tree. With this experience, he became an awakened one who embodied deep inner peace, genuine wisdom, and overflowing compassion. This inner transformation that occurred in him was palpable to those around him, and exuded through all his words and deeds, thus attracting people to him as they sought his guidance on how they too, might become, like him, awakened.

And the good news is that we—you and I—are also invited to see and realize that world for ourselves, and to know that it can transform our own lives and how we relate to one another and to everything else. The Chan tradition is a school of Buddhist practice that invites people to "taste and see" this world, offering practical pointers in this direction. This is the Buddha's own invitation, cached in his response to individuals' questions about how to get to where he had arrived, referred to as the "place of peace" (*santam padam*) in early scriptural texts. Many words are recorded as coming out of his mouth in response to these questions, but his most simple and direct response is summed up in this invitation: "Come and see!" (*Ehi passiko* in Pāli.)

The author of this book, Ben Connelly, a Zen teacher and Dharma heir in the Katagiri lineage, reaffirms the invitation for us, offering a set of pointers that can open us to a view of that glorious world of enlightenment depicted in the *Flower Garland Sutra*, taking a set of verses of thirty lines composed by Uisang, a seventh-century Korean monk, as guideposts in the adventure.

The approach of Zen is rather simple, though admittedly not easy by any means, as those who have taken it up can attest. It invites us to take a three-step movement. First, take a posture conducive to stillness, usually a seated position, but it may also be while walking, standing, or some other posture that enables a silencing of the mind and heart. Second, breathe with attention, not letting the monkey mind hold sway but rather bringing the mind and heart back to the breath each time we notice ourselves wandering off. And thirdly, let the mind and heart come home to the here and now, bask in the stillness, and dwell therein. Here, time and space are no more, and there is only that stillness that opens out to a vast and infinite horizon.

Dwelling in this stillness, at the still point of the turning world, to borrow from poet T. S. Eliot, the vast and infinite, wondrous universe of the *Flower Garland Sutra* can open up to us *in this very body*. The moment this happens, we realize that *here* is *home*. Exploring and coursing through the vast, infinite universe, we realize we never left home, and are amazed, our hearts filled with peace and untold joy. This is a peace and joy we cannot help but want to share with everyone in the world.

Those who are drawn to an exploration of this unfathomable realm are invited to follow those three steps outlined above—it may also help to join a sangha or community of practice, and seek the guidance of a teacher who has been there, done that—and remain steadfast and assiduous in the practice, cultivating and dwelling in stillness. Come and see!

And again, with thanks to T. S. Eliot,

We shall not cease from exploration
and the end of all our exploring
will be to arrive where we started
and know the place for the first time.

Waking up in one's own home, however, one opens one's eyes and realizes that the household is in disarray. One's own children are lost in mindless play or are busy fighting one another, the stronger ones lording it over the others, who are left with little to survive on. All is not well. To top all this, fires are raging in different places, threatening the collapse of the house itself. With new eyes, one comes to realize, *this is my home*, and I cannot just sit smugly and allow all this suffering to go unattended.

The pilgrim Sudhana, having neared the end of his journey in meeting his first teacher, Manjusri, is then led to the bodhisattva Samantabhadra, who teaches him a final lesson. All the wisdom learned along the way would not be complete unless it is put into compassionate action, in manifold ways, in repairing this broken home.

Ruben L. F. Habito
Santa Fe, New Mexico

Introduction

Under a vaulted ceiling in the radiance of stained glass, I met Professor Jin Park at Augsburg University chapel in Minneapolis. She was visiting from American University to give a talk called "Ethical Imagination," which wove a warp of Huayan and Yogacara Buddhism with a weft of contemporary movements for liberation. Inspired by her talk, I approached her and confided the particular challenge I was facing. I wanted to write a practical book about Huayan (Flower Garland) Buddhism based on a short, comprehensive text, but I couldn't find a classic text that fit my aspirations. She immediately offered inspiration: the Korean master Uisang's "Ocean Seal Chart." As those red, yellow, and green panels of stained glass opened the sky to the chapel at Augsburg, so too has Uisang's song opened a way to the vast spacious dimensions of Huayan. I am deeply grateful for the Dharma and for Dr. Park's insight and friendly encouragement to move this project forward at a few key moments when it was starting to slip away.

The Flower Garland Buddhist tradition is relational, practical, and positive. Arising fifteen hundred years ago, it has made a deep impact on East Asian Buddhism, and has much to offer during this era when many folks see ever-deepening divisions. Huayan offers particular wisdom for those concerned about how to care for their own lives as they work to end harms such as ecological devastation, poverty, militarism, addiction, marginalization, and exploitation. I was originally called to study Huayan by reading Thich Nhat Hanh's teachings, which draw deeply from Huayan to form his vision for what has become known as engaged Buddhism. I frequently see the Huayan worldview reflected in ecological thought. Robin Wall Kimmerer quotes Joanna Macy in *Braiding Sweetgrass*, which celebrates the indigenous North American tradition of mutual support among people and plants. Her words could have come straight from a Huayan text: "Action on behalf of life transforms. Because the relationship between self and the world is reciprocal, it is not a question of first getting enlightened or saved and then acting. As we work to heal the earth, the earth heals us."[1]

This book provides a broad overview of the Flower Garland Sutra and Huayan teachings and their practical implications for contemporary life. Each chapter is a commentary on one of the thirty lines in Uisang's Ocean Seal Chart. Much of the source material for this book is other Huayan and Buddhist texts, but I also draw on a diverse array of voices from contemporary life. I have provided endnotes with citations for those seeking further study, but there are no explanatory notes. In some cases, I quote something I received through oral transmission, and no citation is provided. As a Westerner trained in the Japanese Soto Zen tradition, I aspire to approach this project with cultural humility. Uisang's text has been a deeply embedded part of the lives of Korean people for over a thousand years. I thank the Korean people—academics, monastics, and lay folks—who helped me understand how they relate to and understand this text, and humbly pray that this book will honor their practice, their lives, and their understanding.

Avatamsaka Sutra

Huayan, (literally "Flower Garland," Korean: Hwaeom, Japanese: Kegon) Buddhism arose in China in the sixth century CE. It takes its name and its themes from the Indian *Avatamsaka*, or *Flower Garland, Sutra*. It puts great emphasis on teachings of interdependence, and thus on the value and importance of each and every aspect of our phenomenal world: the flowers, the people in all their diversity, the animals, meals, gardens, soil, labors, sufferings, and loves. Many Buddhist teachings invite us to become free by letting go of things, the *Avatamsaka Sutra* invites us to see a world so abundant that we don't feel a need to hold on to anything.

Although the Huayan school calls itself an *ekayana*, or "one vehicle," tradition that affirms the value of all Buddhist schools, Huayan texts also show how it is distinct from the others. It puts less emphasis on the individual path of attaining nirvana than the Early Buddhist schools.

It relies less on negative rhetoric than the early Mahayana literature such as Prajnaparamita texts and Madhyamaka philosophy. It is less psychological than the Yogacara teachings. And yet, it includes all these within its jeweled web. Huayan philosophy is relentless, abundant, and joyous in its ornate literary expressions of the wonder of each moment. It celebrates that all individual things are but manifestations of something yet more vast and amazing: the universe, the Dharma realm, a place where our practice and how we treat each thing always matters.

The style of the *Avatamsaka Sutra*, by far the longest Buddhist sutra at fifteen hundred pages, is surely intended to blow the mind, with its lists of hundreds of radiantly named bodhisattvas, its ornate descriptions of jeweled banners, vast crowds of magnificent beings, palaces, forests, practices, and mountains. Because the sutra is so vast as to defy summarization, we will use the Huayan teachings it inspired along with many quotations from the sutra itself to enter its wonders. The *Avatamsaka* and the Huayan teachings that take it as their base are in many ways quite different from the Early Buddhist teachings. However, we can see seeds of the Huayan emphasis on appreciation for the sensual world and the diversity of people and practices in the earliest Buddhist texts. In the *Mahagosinga Sutta* of the Pali Canon, we find many of the Buddha's main disciples gathered in intimate conversation. Each one says, "the Gosinga Sala tree wood [forest] is delightful, the night is moonlit, the sala trees are all in blossom, and heavenly scents seem to be floating in the air. What kind of bhikku [monastic], friend . . . could illuminate the Gosinga Salatree Wood?"[2] They rejoice in the natural beauty, and ask what practice could possibly augment it. Each disciple—Ananda, Revata, Anuruddha, Maha Kassapa, Moggallana, and Sariputra—shares their particular vision for practice: memorizing teachings, solitary meditation, using the divine eye to see a thousand worlds, harmonizing words and actions, meeting face to face in Dharma dialogue, and abiding in deep meditation states. Then the Buddha arrives, they share their various views with him, and they ask which is best. He says that each method is complete. He also adds his own: to commit oneself to freedom from suffering through mindfulness and chosen poverty.

There are various versions of the *Avatamsaka Sutra* arising around the middle of the first millennium CE. Some of its chapters were originally circulated as standalone sutras before the whole text was compiled. Three appeared early on and were particularly influential on Huayan thought: the *Ten Stages*, *Purifying Practice*,[3] and the *Gandavyuha* sutras.

The *Ten Stages Sutra* is a mind-blowing account of the bodhisattva's path of ever-deepening practice. Each stage includes wondrous spiritual attainments, which open ever onward into deeper compassion and joy. We find this sutra referred to in Buddhist texts from many different traditions.

The *Purifying Practice Sutra* comprises about a hundred

and fifty verses. In each one the practitioner is invited to bring the wish that all beings be free from suffering to a specific activity: walking, shaving, entering a room, getting dressed, meditating, bathing, taking refuge in Buddha. Although Huayan is philosophically complex, the philosophy is rooted in an invitation to awaken our hearts to all beings in each particular activity and relationship. Here are a few of the verses:

> When seeing a park,
> He should vow: "May all beings
> Diligently cultivate all the practices
> And progress toward the bodhi of the Buddha."[4]

. . . .

> When seeing an empty bowl,
> He should vow: "May all beings
> Have minds that are pure and empty
> Of all the afflictions."
>
> When seeing a bowl that is full,
> He should vow: "May all beings
> Completely fulfill
> All of the good dharmas."[5]

The refuge vows that are a part of the daily chanting service in Soto Zen temples' verses are found in the *Purifying Practice Sutra*:

I take refuge in Buddha
May all living beings
embody the great way,
resolving to awaken.

I take refuge in Dharma
May all living beings
deeply enter the sutras,
wisdom like an ocean.

I take refuge in Sangha
May all living beings
support harmony in the community,
free from hindrance.[6]

Over time these verses have evolved, and rather than simply containing a wish that people be free from suffering, they are sometimes translated to include a vow to free them. Here is an adapted verse composed by Thich Nhat Hanh:

Waking up this morning, I smile.
Twenty-four brand new hours are before me.
I vow to live fully in each moment
and to look at all beings with eyes of compassion[7]

The *Gandavyuha Sutra*, or *Entry Into the Realm of Reality Sutra*, is the third of the key standalone sutras that were incorporated into the *Avatamsaka*. It constitutes the final and longest chapter of the *Avatamsaka Sutra*. It tells the story of a young man, Sudhana, who commits his life to liberation from suffering for everyone and everything, and of his long and wondrous pilgrimage on the path. He meets with fifty-three teachers, each of whom shows him a staggering level of spiritual attainment, and then ends their meeting by saying they can't possibly know the way to liberation. Each one sends him on to visit another teacher, to keep practicing. The teachers include beggars, queens, boys and girls, monks, nuns, rich men, mathematicians, sailors, perfumers, goddesses, bark-clad outcasts, folks who change genders, people dressed in rags, those bedecked in jewels, a prince who almost loses his life working to free all the prisoners in his land, and great bodhisattvas: Avalokiteshvara, Manjusri, and Samtantabhadra. They teach in myriad ways, all different and appropriate to themselves and those they meet: they teach by feeding people, through physical touch, by making beautiful scents and palaces, by writing, by teaching meditation, by expounding the Dharma, by revealing suffering, and by guiding people through storms. This sutra provides inspiration for those of us looking to create multicultural, engaged Buddhist communities.

The story of the *Gandavyuha* resonates still today. There are temples in East Asia that include a series of images or altars representing teachers Sudhana visited on his pilgrimage, so practitioners may embody his voyage in ritual space as they move from image to image. In 1991, the poet and monk Ko Un published a bestselling novel in Korea named *Little Pilgrim*, which retells the story of Sudhana. The novel is a wonderful invitation into the dreamlike landscape of the sutra and the path of liberation.

In East Asian Buddhist traditions, the *Avatamsaka* is often understood to have been the first teaching of the Buddha, but historians say its first sections arose about five hundred years after the death of the historical Buddha. In sixth-century China, the great Tiantai teacher Zhiyi compared it to the sunrise, which is first seen only on the highest mountain peaks. Not everyone is ready to climb into this rarified air, and some of us may wait for the light to come down into the valleys or set across the western horizon. It is a monumental read. The great Korean master Chinul wrote, "Because the treatise is . . . too lengthy and expansive, it was difficult for me to expound it. . . . Nevertheless it is the best mirror of the mind for sentient beings of great mind who enter the gate of complete-sudden (Hwaeom) enlightenment."[8] Like many East Asian Buddhist schools, Huayan associates itself with an Indian text, but one does not need to read the root text to study Huayan.

I have found studying and chanting the *Avatamsaka* to be quite wondrous. For those of you who are interested, I recommend starting with one of the three sections I described above. I learned to study sutras sitting in a circle of my peers after morning meditation with my teacher Tim

Burkett guiding us with probing questions. We would sometimes use one of the simplest and best ways to dive into this sutra literature, which I call "samadhi reading." When I first read the *Gandavyuha*,[9] I committed to reading fifteen minutes per day. Each day, I would read aloud from the sutra without pause or reflection. I gave my full attention to the experience of the reading, and then trusted the rest. Although I was sometimes bored, annoyed, or grasping, ultimately I found this practice deepened my sense of the mystery and connection that is always vividly present in every moment of experience. I recall Norman Fischer's joy as he recounted a ceremony at San Francisco Zen Center's Green Gulch Farm where a large group of people was chanting from the *Avatamsaka* as a chorus of frogs joined in, and the temple's many bells rang in harmony. Here is just a taste of the *Gandavyuha*:

> At that time, Sudhana the Youth aroused thoughts of the highest esteem toward the good spiritual guide, developed a vast and pure conviction, always remained mindful of the Great Vehicle, focused on seeking the Buddha's wisdom, and yearned to see the buddhas. . . . His mind was free of any discriminations among all buddhas. He had destroyed the net of the many mental conceptions, had abandoned all attachments, refrained from seizing on any buddha's congregations, and also refrained from seiz-

> ing on the Buddha's pure land. He realized all beings have no self, realized all sounds are like echoes, and realized all forms are like reflected images. He then gradually traveled south until he reached the city of Simhavijrimbhita where he searched all around for Maitrayani.[10]

The townspeople told him the girl Maitrayani, daughter of the rajah Simhaketu, surrounded by five hundred girls, was on the roof of the palace of shining jewels, on a sandalwood seat draped with nets of jewels and heavenly cloth, offering teaching. "Hearing this, Sudhana entered the city, went to the house of the rajah, and stood at the outer foyer, desirous of seeing the girl Maitrayani. There he saw hundreds of thousands of people going in. He asked them where they were going and why they had come, and they told him they were going to Maitrayani to hear the Teaching. He thought to himself, 'No one is prevented from going in.' So he went in."[11]

Great Huayan and Hwaeom Teachers

Huayan is often associated with five eminent Chinese monks from the sixth through the ninth centuries CE: Dushun, Zhiyan, Fazang, Chengguan, and Guifeng Zongmi. Their Huayan is reflected in many Chan and subsequent Japanese Zen teachings, and in fact, Guifeng Zongmi is considered one of the great Chan (Zen) ancestors as well. (These men are often referred to as *patriarchs* in the literature. I do not wish to downplay the fact that Buddhism has been characterized by a painful degree of patriarchy, but I will not use this term in this book, except in quotations.)

The Huayan tradition was transmitted to Korea in the seventh century—where it became Hwaeom—by two Korean colleagues, Uisang and Wonhyo. These two traveled through war-torn territory to study and transmit the Dharma. Uisang is the author of the "Song of Dharma Nature" on which this book is a commentary. He studied with Zhiyan in China, and both he and Wonhyo were peers of Fazang. The historical record of the lives of these monks is scanty, but the varied traditional accounts of their path to Huayan shows their powerful place in the Korean collective imagination.

Wonhyo and Uisang attempted the dangerous trek to China to meet great Buddhist teachers. In the midst of the arduous journey, deep in the night, desperate with thirst, Wonhyo found a large mug full of refreshing spring water and drank deeply. When they woke in the morning, he saw that the mug was a skull full of brackish mud. Wonhyo's mind opened to the Buddhist teaching that phenomena arise dependent on mind and thus saw no reason to travel to China to study. Uisang carried on his pilgrimage alone.

Stories say that Uisang stayed with a devout family on his journey. A daughter, Seonmyo, fell in love with him. Uisang made clear that as a celibate monk, he could not requite her affections, and she decided to devote her life to his protection. Through her commitment, she became able to transform into a dragon. As a dragon, she guided his ship from China through a storm, and in Korea, she transformed into a huge boulder that still protects the gate at Pusok-sa, "Temple of Floating Stone," which Uisang founded.[12] Uisang was a born aristocrat and became a powerful and well-connected figure in Silla—the reigning dynasty in Korea at that time. He founded several large temples that are still operating and influential today. He was also known for promoting people of all classes as teachers within his community. They say the king once offered him a house with accompanying servants. He declined, saying "My dharma teaches equality, there is no distinction between high and low class, and anybody can share it. The *Mahaparinirvana-sutra* says that we should not possess any property which has been unfairly gained. What is the use of land and for what do I need servants? The dharma world is my house, and I have bowls for food. I live relying on the wisdom of the Buddha."[13]

Writing about one of Uisang's only extant texts, the subject of this book, Mu Soeng Sunim writes, "All the subsequent systematizers of Korean Buddhism relied heavily on Uisang's schematic chart of the *Avatamsaka Sutra* and quoted copiously from it. Through the efforts of Uisang and his disciples, Hwaeom (Avatamsaka) became the cutting edge of all future doctrinal developments in Korean Buddhism."[14]

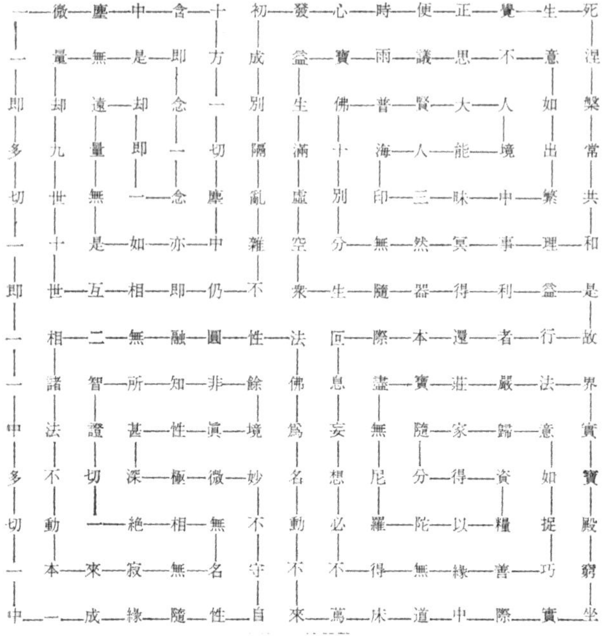

Seal of the Huayan One Vehicle Dharma Realm

The "Song of Dharma Nature" consists of thirty lines, each with seven classical Chinese characters. These characters are arranged into a maze-like grid, called variously Hwaeom Ilseung Beopkye Do, Beopseongge, the Seal of the Huayan One Vehicle Dharma Realm, Haein Do, or Ocean Seal Chart. Like a rolling wheel of Dharma, the characters of the poem begin in the middle of the diagram and through a winding path make their way in a general clockwise motion to arrive again in the middle, where it all began.[15] The chapters of this book provide commentary on each line of this diagram's text, which I will refer to by its many names.

Along with the text and the diagram in which it is embedded, Uisang created a line-by-line commentary on the text. Some scholars contend that the poem itself may have been composed by Uisang's teacher Zhiyan; however, this is not a widely accepted idea. Similar debates have occurred in the case of other influential Buddhist texts—for example, some say that the "Song of the Jewel Mirror Samadhi" attributed to Dongshan may have been "his" only because it was transmitted to him by his teacher Yunyan. Uisang does little to dispel doubts about authorship. In his commentary on the text he writes: "Why do you [I] not show the name of the author? Answer: It is because I would show that all dharmas produced by causes have no such thing as a host."[16] Over and again these teachers will demonstrate that Dharma is not something owned or grasped, but a relational process.

The Seal Diagram touches on many of the central themes of the Huayan tradition and provides us many entry points into this wondrous teaching. It takes as its source the *Avatamsaka* (*Flower Garland*) *Sutra*, and provides a terse, memorable entry into the wisdom and vision of that vast text. It is a compact expression of this deep well of Dharma. In his commentary on the Seal, Uisang refers to the *Avatamsaka* and *Srimaladevi* sutras, the *Awakening of Faith*, to Vasubandhu's commentary on the *Ten Stages Sutra*, and to Asanga's great Yogacara Buddhist text, the *Mahayanasamgraha* (*A Compendium of the Mahayana*).

Of the winding path the poem makes through the Seal Diagram, Uisang writes that the one path represents the one sound of the Buddha, and the twists and turns represent the diversity of capacities and needs of the countless beings with which we share this earth.[17] Of the weaving lines of poetry he writes, "No matter how far you go, you are in the original place, and no matter whether you arrive, you are in the place of departure."[18] In some ways, the Seal Diagram resembles a mandala, but although its path winds from end to beginning in an endless circle, the shape is square. Uisang writes that the four sides of the diagram represent the bodhisattva's four methods of guidance, which permeate the first chapter of the *Avatamsaka*: giving, kind speech, beneficial action, and cooperation. The four corners represent the four immeasurable aspects of mind: loving-kindness, compassion, sympathetic joy, and equanimity.[19] The path of the poem through the diagram is also a symbolic map of the path of Sudhana's pilgrimage in the final chapter of the *Avatamsaka*. Uisang writes, "One day someone fell asleep and dreamt that he was wandering about thirty places. When he awoke, he found that he was lying in the same position as he had started in, without changing. In this way, though we start from the first character 'Dharma' [in the diagram] and return to that same character, passing all others along the way, it is in the same position as if we had never moved at all."[20]

This Seal Diagram has been a subject of study, devotion, and reverence for a long time. For many people this Seal

Diagram is an object of great spiritual power. I recently found a video[21] of a large crowd of lay people walking a slow winding path through the courtyard of Songgwangsa temple in Korea to the sound of bells, chanting, and birdsong. They were walking the route of a giant labyrinth imprinted on the ground, a massive version of the Seal Diagram of the Huayan One Vehicle Dharma Realm. Professor Chang-Seong Hong described the same style of chanting and meditative walking done at Haein-sa Monastery to me, then casually mentioned, "I've done it hundreds of times." The "Song of Dharma Nature" is chanted in Korean funeral rites and used as a spell to gain the fulfillment of wishes. The Seal Diagram is often used as a protective amulet.[22] Korean Buddhists understand its use in many different ways. Recently, I asked the Korean nun Sinwoo Sunim via email about the Ocean Seal Chart. She offered me these words on the contemporary use of our text in Korean Buddhism: "Everyday ceremony usually ends by chanting the Ocean Seal Chart. The Ocean Seal Chart is an extract-like sentence that contains all the truth, so beginners unconditionally study, memorize, and recite it every day. . . . You start your day at home by reciting the Ocean Seal Chart and thinking deeply about its meaning." I encourage you to take up chanting or reciting the text as an aspect of your engagement with this book.

This book will emphasize how to practice a life of liberation informed by the "Song of Dharma Nature." It was created to be part of Huayan practice, which includes taking refuge in the three treasures—the Buddha, Dharma, and Sangha—following the precepts, and practicing meditation.

To take refuge in the Buddha, Dharma, and Sangha is an act of devotion. It is a way to find a sense of safety and support, to surrender our habitual ways of seeking refuge that do not actually help, and to turn toward refuge in the interdependence—the intimacy—of all things.

Five precepts underlie all the many different lists of precepts in the various Buddhist traditions: to refrain from killing, lying, stealing, using intoxicants, and misusing sexuality. The precise way one enacts these precepts varies, but from a Buddhist perspective they are essential to ending suffering and the cause of suffering. To practice the precepts is to always consider how to maintain them more deeply, and to embody the vision that flows from our contemplation.

Meditation can be practiced in many ways. Huayan calls itself one vehicle, which means it includes the whole array of Buddhist traditions and meditation practices. We will explore various approaches to meditation in this book, but here I will say that the meaning of these words will flower in the light of meditation if you let it. I invite you to find time every day to sit upright and know the feelings in the body, the sensations in the belly as the body breathes, to know emotions as they arise and pass away, to hear the breeze, the car alarms, the rustling leaves, to watch the light deepen at dawn and the dark deepen at dusk. I pray that you may trust this, and entrust yourself to it.

• • • • •

In seventeenth-century China, the nun Kedu wrote this verse that carries forth the great flowering of the Huayan.

> Drop off the body, the river of the world will never end,
> Stately and grand: nothing to show but the inner
> master.
> When morning comes, change the water, light the
> incense,
> Everything is in the ordinary affairs of the everyday
> world.[23]

To drop off the body is not to throw it away, but to entrust it, as one drops off a child at a grandparent's house. The "Song of Dharma Nature" invites us to find refuge in the river of the world, the ever-flowing sights, sounds, smells, emotions, thoughts, bodily sensations, and tastes. To see that the whole world is here in this moment, in how we care for what is here right now.

Song of Dharma Nature

華嚴一乘法界圖

法性圓融無二相
諸法不動本來寂
無名無相絶一切
證智所知非餘境
眞性甚深極微妙
不守自性隨緣成

一中一切多中一
一卽一切多卽一
一微塵中含十方
一切塵中亦如是
無量遠劫卽一念
一念卽是無量劫
九世十世互相卽
仍不雜亂隔別成
初發心時便正覺
生死涅槃常共和
理事冥然無分別

十佛普賢大人境

能仁海印三昧中
繁出如意不思議

雨寶益生滿虛空

Seal of the Huayan One Vehicle Dharma Realm By Uisang, translated by Ben Connelly and Weijen Teng

Dharma nature is all-pervading harmony, without duality.
All dharmas are unmoving, fundamentally peaceful.
Without name, without characteristic, cutting through all,
It is known in realized wisdom, not in another realm.
True nature is so very profound, minutely subtle;
Not attached to self nature, it arises dependent on conditions.
Within one is all, within many is one.
One is all, the many are one.
Within one mote of dust is contained the ten directions.
Within each phenomenon it is also thus.
Immeasurable distant eons are one moment of mind;
One moment of mind is immeasurable eons.
The nine times and the ten times are mutually identical,
Yet not mixed or disordered, they arise separately.
The mind's first aspiration for awakening is true awakening.
Life-and-death and nirvana are always identical;
Universal and particulars are thus unfathomable, not distinct.
This is the realm of the ten buddhas and Samantabhadra, the great ones.
In the midst of Buddha's Ocean Seal samadhi,
The abundant manifestations of wish fulfillment are inconceivable.
This rain of jewels benefits all life, filling all space.

衆生隨器得利益
是故行者還本際
破息妄想必不得
無緣善巧捉如意
歸家隨分得資糧
以陀羅尼無盡寶
莊嚴法界實寶殿
窮坐實際中道床

舊來不動名爲佛

All beings benefit according to their capacities.
Thus the practitioner returns to the true source.
Without ending delusion it is surely not attained.
Unconditional skillful means bring wish fulfillment.
Returning home, effortlessly gaining treasures,
Through dharani, an inexhaustible treasure
Adorns the Dharma realm, a true jeweled palace.
Just sitting in the bed of the Middle Way, the ultimate reality,
This original stillness is named Buddha.

1

The Round Teaching

法性圓融無二相

Dharma nature is all-pervading harmony, without duality.

Everything, every place, and everyone is suffused with compassion, harmony, and wholeness: the birds I hear conversing in the spring dawn light, the feeling of air moving through my body, in and out, the aching hearts of my loved ones, and all those I am too ignorant to love. This lofty, comforting, mystifying idea is where Uisang begins.

Dharma is an ancient word. It means many things: truth, teaching, phenomenon, reality. In Buddhist thought it is deeply associated with the ideas that there is suffering, that you can do something about it, and that suffering can be completely left behind. The teaching of Dharma is that which promotes this truth. Dharma, or truth, in Buddhist thought does not refer to apparently objective truths but to what buddhas see: what is known by those who are awake, who don't suffer, don't cause suffering, and who help folks be free from suffering. Buddhas help people see the harmony that they see. While Early Buddhist teachings emphasize the path from suffering to nonsuffering, from samsara to nirvana, Mahayana teachings emphasize that samsara and nirvana are inseparable. They are both here now. The Dharma that is the end of suffering is reality. The compassion that the Buddha embodied is never separate from this moment, and in fact is simply seeing that it isn't separate. It's not an object apart from you. It isn't somewhere else, some other time, some other better person. This is it!

Personally, I find this a difficult entry point into the teachings, having been raised with a humanistic, scientific worldview. I am attracted to Buddhist teachings that start with something a little more plain to see, for example "there is suffering," and slowly build the argument that nirvana is already here. In the earliest layer of Buddhist teachings, the Pali Canon, the Buddha reserves teachings on the unconditioned nature of nirvana for advanced practitioners at particularly inspired moments.[24] However, I well recall the startling, utterly disarming moment when a Zen teacher first said to me, "You are Buddha." The tears pouring from my eyes, the shame suffusing my body from years of addiction and trauma, and my desperate need to be something else, were cracked open in a moment, with a woman in black Buddhist robes embodying a vast compassion that was right in front of me, and suddenly and viscerally within me.

I have made thousands of bows to altars at Zen temples and offered clouds of incense and flower petals. Morning after morning, I have chanted my profound appreciation for the Buddha and the great teachers of the Buddhist tradition, but devotional practice is still not very natural for me. I felt something new on a recent trip to Vietnam. I entered many temples and made bows to huge statues of Buddhas with Vietnamese folks, who radiated an unforced reverence for the awesome power of the Buddha, a faith in the Dharma that he taught. The collective feeling that the Buddha and Dharma were incomprehensibly powerful, pervasive, and compassionate was electric. This devotion and faith is the power Uisang invokes by starting this song with the word *Dharma*.

The *Flower Ornament Sutra* says "The buddhas practice this way: Nothing can be grasped."[25] If this teaching seems hard to get a handle on, that's not surprising. The point is that it is not a thing, separate from other things that we can get, hold, figure out, or attain. We translate the Chinese characters 圓融 as "all-pervading harmony" in this context. They could also be translated, respectively, as "round, interfused." Things that are round roll. They are not held in place. They have no edges. Things that are interfused can't be held. You can't hold the water that is in a washcloth, that suffuses the air and your own hands as you wash a baby—who is also mostly water—in a little tub. Yet wheels are quite helpful, and the care we give is a miracle.

I recently heard a talk by a Mohican teacher, Reverend Jim Bear Jacobs. He asked someone to name the cardinal directions. Someone (likely of European descent) called out "north, south, east, and west." Jim Bear pointed out that in his culture the directions form a circle, not a set of dualistic opposites: east, south, west, and north. The Dharma nature, too, is round, not dualistic; it flows and rolls. Often Korean texts will refer to their tradition as "the round teaching."[26]

For those of you familiar with other Buddhist teachings, you may notice that the idea of Dharma nature, which is a particular innovation of the Huayan tradition, is deeply tied to the Early Buddhist teachings on the unconditioned, on Mahayana teachings on Prajnaparamita, emptiness, and the absolute, and to the Yogacara idea that things are of complete, realized natures. These Huayan teachings take a positive approach, emphasizing that all the harmony that the Buddha brought to the community is here right now. This approach pervades later East Asian Buddhist traditions. Dogen Zenji begins his *Universal Recommendation for Zazen* (*Fukanzazengi*) thus: "The Way is originally perfect and all pervading. . . ." There are myriad ways to help us all see our total dependence on each other. This text invites us to hear that the harmony, all the different notes, the dissonance and resonances, are also one unbroken whole.

A few years ago I was at a camp formed by Indigenous women to stop the construction of an oil pipeline on Anishinaabe land near the headwaters of the Mississippi. Standing in the path of the pipeline on the bank of the mighty river, we sang. I heard voices in harmony, the songs of birds, the relentless grinding roar of a massive drill driving the pipeline under the Mississippi River, and the wind in the trees above the water. For a few moments I heard it all as harmony.

The Dharma nature, this perfectly interfused harmony, is without duality. Its basic characteristic is roundness, which here also implies completeness, interfusion, and nonduality. The Chinese term 無二, (*wu er*, or *advaya* in Sanskrit) means "nonduality." Many Buddhist teachings from the time of the *Avatamsaka* and the rise of Huayan Buddhism point out that any particular way of seeing things as dual (for example, self-other, life-death, water-washcloth, north-south, form-emptiness) does not reflect an absolute truth, but just a conditioned way of seeing things formed by our habits of body and mind. The truth, the Dharma, is that our dualistic way of seeing things is not the whole picture. Our belief in the absoluteness of these things that are not absolute causes our suffering.

In a ninth-century commentary on this first line of the "Song of Dharma Nature," Pobyung writes: "What is 'dharma'? . . . [I]t is precisely your body and mind. What is 'nature'? It is perfect interfusion. What is 'perfect interfusion'? It is called that because it does not possess the characteristic of duality."[27]

Your body and mind are not separate. They are not separate from each other. They are not separate from the earth, the trees, the rivers, rains, or oceans. They are not separate from all the vast wisdom and compassion of the Buddha, and the profound peace that he taught and embodied. But perhaps this does not ring true to you, for I have created a duality between non-separation and the apparent separations we usually see. This duality I have made also isn't real. However you feel and perceive things right now, even if it is through countless dualities, is fully affirmed in nonduality. It's not something else.

2

Peace in the Present

諸法不動本來寂

All dharmas are unmoving, fundamentally peaceful.

In an ancient Buddhist story, the Buddha hears of a notorious mass murder named Angulimala and heads into the wilds to meet him. The murderer, seeing the monk, runs to catch and slay him. The Buddha walks slowly and calmly, but Angulimala never gets any nearer. Angulimala cries out, "Stop." The Buddha, still walking, says, "I have stopped, Angulimala, you stop too." Angulimala sheds his violent ways and devotes himself to peace and humility.[28]

I was sitting in a hard backed chair in an addiction treatment intake interview nonchalantly explaining what a badass I was. The pressure I was under to enter rehabilitation had not tempered my disdain for the process and the changes it hoped to make in my life. I bragged and I postured. The counselor, Connie, put down her pad and paper, took a deep breath, looked me in the eye and asked,

"Can we just stop?" It was then that the tears poured down my face and a door to a new life opened.

This second verse of our text makes a pivot that is common in Huayan, between universal and particular. In the first line, Uisang says the Dharma nature pervades everything, and in this second line, that each particular dharma is peaceful. Here Uisang highlights that the word *dharma* means "phenomenon." The Buddhist Abhidharma tradition provides a detailed account of how to relate to the particular phenomena in each moment of experience. It is based on mindfulness of the body, of sensory experience, and of the emotions and thoughts that motivate us to act. For many of us, mindfulness and meditation practices allow us to see the myriad things of the present moment as a constant flow, and to let it pass without being so upset and driven by it. This makes space for us to choose our actions from our values and our vows rather than our habits. Uisang's verse here speaks to a rarer and perhaps deeper experience. We can see that each thing is entirely and wholly itself only right now. It didn't come from the past and isn't going anywhere. It's not making things happen. It's just still. Sometimes, during a break on a long retreat at our Zen center, folks will be sitting on the porch facing out toward the windows. The crowdedness of our small building and the jitteriness of the early days of retreat both seem to fade as the bodies of the people in the room exude a profound stillness, as though they are not people sitting in chairs or walking to the tea table but stones of the earth or trees gently waving.

This line of the text is a paraphrase of a line in the first Yogacara Buddhist sutra, the *Samdhinirmocana*, which says, "All phenomena are unproduced, unceasing, quiescent from the start and naturally in a state of nirvana."[29] This idea pervades Mahayana Buddhist thought; each thing is nirvana, and is also inseparable from samsara. This is not a denial of the importance of your suffering or that of others; rather, it is a different way of seeing that enables us to engage in acts to alleviate suffering from a grounding in stillness and peace.

Since Dharma nature pervades everything, each thing is peace. This claim that each thing is unmoving arises from the direct experience of countless Buddhists, and is often explained with Mahayana philosophy and analogy. Imagine a river in flood, rushing high above its usual banks. We would usually say this river is moving and destructive. But let's imagine a point on the river where we see it clawing at the bank, pulling chunks of mud into the current. In a single moment we can see that the water sweeping the mud away is made by our way of seeing. An interaction of dualistic assumptions makes it seem like there is movement: the bank is a lasting thing separate from the water, the river has a lasting nature separate from each moment of flow, the rain that fed the flood is separate from the river, we are separate from the bank and from the river, the past is separate from the present and the future. It is possible for there to be mere experience of the moment of what we would conventionally call mud, water, and seeing, without all these assumptions. It is possible for each thing to be known exactly and only now, unmoving. Seeing this stillness is seeing a peace that is never separate from this moment. It is always available to you, and in a sense, always how things actually are whether you know it or not.

On the day the verdict in the trial of Derek Chauvin was announced, there was a mass gathering at George Floyd Square near my home in Minneapolis. Many of my colleagues prepared an interfaith vigil to help our community process enormous waves of emotion, and to move forward in the possibility of liberation from racism and police brutality. Another group of colleagues, the BIPOC Sanghas for Direct Action, convened a group of about thirty people to sit in meditation in the midst of the throng of thousands. As the roaring chants, the songs, the lament, and celebration poured from the crowd, these few folks were also there, inseparable from the whole, embodying a stillness and peace that any one of us could also have seen everywhere we looked.

3

Cutting Through It All

無名無相絶一切

Without name, without characteristic, cutting through all,

I have seen tears streaming down the faces of folks chanting the *Heart Sutra*, arguably the most central ceremonial text of the Mahayana tradition. The faces were in a video of a mass gathering in Japan, but I have also been in many smaller rooms with folks across the United States and abroad pouring our energy into this chanting, this worship of Prajnaparamita. Prajnaparamita, the perfection of wisdom, is the awareness that there are no things, no characteristics, no names that can fully hold the mystery of a moment. There is nothing to hold on to, and realizing this cuts through the whole web that binds us, opening us to a liberated encounter with everything.

Here our text says the Dharma nature that pervades everything, and all the individual dharmas—that is, phenomena—are not bound by the names we give them, and don't ultimately have the characteristics we ascribe to them. Even the all-pervasiveness, the nonduality, and the peacefulness the text says they have in the first two lines aren't ultimately real. The *Avatamsaka Sutra* says bodhisattvas "do not create duality in things / nor do they create nonduality / They are free of duality and nonduality / realizing they are just manners of speaking."[30] Buddhists, who have created great libraries of literature, celebrate speaking and writing, but in the Mahayana we also emphasize the limitations of words, the non-absoluteness of truths that we find in words, and the wonder of letting words go to cut through all distinctions.

In one of the earliest Huayan texts, Dushun wrote, "All dharmas are inexpressible. [Indeed] their [very] inexpressibility is inexpressible. Even these words do not apply! [True emptiness] is really transcendent and quite without support. It is nothing which words can reach, nor anything which explanations can attain. And this [in turn] means that it [belongs properly] to the realm of practice."[31] Put simply, because we can't control things and they are beyond our words, this is the most important thing: what are you doing right now?

Yesterday, at a meeting at our Zen center, we were talking about how to celebrate and support the vast array of Zen practices in order to promote an inclusive community. Folks named flower arranging, walking meditation, sweeping, zazen, writing poetry, cleaning toilets, deep listening, textual study, hospitality, sewing, cooking, socializing, gardening, chanting, rituals, calligraphy, singing, and more—and then one of our elders said, "Silence." She spoke of the vast space of healing and connection she found when she entered retreat under the guidance of Katagiri Roshi, our founder, and learned to not speak, to let the word-making activity of the mind soften and fade. Zen retreats let us meet a life in community; of cooking, cleaning, caring for altars; of meditation, without words, without naming, without the thick dust of characteristics that language settles on all we see, we hear, and we feel. I have learned much about Huayan from books, but I have learned far more about what it points to in silent retreat.

This line of our text, "Without name, without characteristic, cutting through all," lays out one of the basic Mahayana ideas that provides the framework for Huayan. Everything is empty—empty of the separateness created by our way of looking at things. In the dedicatory verse of his seminal *Fundamental Verses of the Middle Way*, Nagarjuna writes:

> I prostrate to the Perfect Buddha,
> The best of teachers, who taught that
> Whatever is dependently arisen is
> Unceasing, unborn,
> Unannihilated, not permanent,
> Not coming, not going,
> Without distinction, without identity,
> And free from conceptual construction.[32]

Dependent arising, the idea that all things arise dependent on other things, is an essential element of Buddhist thought. Later in this book we'll see how Huayan expands on and celebrates its implications. Here though, Uisang ties the rest of the text to this basic idea: because things are entirely dependent on other things, they are not utterly separate from them, and none of the characteristics we ascribe to them are absolutely real. Nagarjuna's philosophical proofs of the liberating impacts of this view are notoriously complex. At different times, I have seen both the Korean master Pomnyun Sunim and Mingyur Rinpoche teach on this subject when asked for clarification. Each one picked up two flowers and held them up to the questioner. Mingyur Rinpoche asked, "Which is short and which is tall?" The person inquiring gave the obvious answer, for one was clearly much larger. Then the teacher put one of them down and with the remaining flower standing alone, asked, "Is this tall or short?" The questioner always ends up with "It depends."

All characteristics are provisional, based on the current context and on our conditioned way of looking at them. This means that our liberation from suffering and our ability to help others be free are not dependent on some absolute truth we can grab on to. There are many ways. Buddhist teachings offer methods for cutting through our habitual ways of looking at things by using the very mental processes that create them. Silent retreat, for years, months, days, or even minutes, can soften the mental processes that make our conditioned view seem so absolute. Face-to-face teaching encounters and meditation practices can cut through our divisive tendencies or sometimes make space for them to simply fall away

Dushun wrote, "Having no nature means conditionality, and conditionality means there is no inherent nature. . . . What sickness does the practice of such contemplation cure? Answer: It cures the sickness of clinging to elements."[33] Going beyond names and seeing through characteristics is medicine for our attempts to hold on to things. Every smile fades, every toy breaks, the strength of our limbs wanes as the years go on, the things we worked so hard for may not come to be—and if they do, will someday pass away. And yes, we will all one day be like my father, memories, or like his great, great grandfather, forgotten. We can cut through the views that make things seem so separate, and we can meet each moment with a vision that sees beyond a bunch of things to fix, judge, or control. We can see that success and failure, gain and loss, and even life and death are ideas, not absolute truths. Thus, I can fully feel the grief and the joy when memories of my father come, and I can also know that he is as close to me as ever.

4

Only Knowing

證智所知非餘境

It is known in realized wisdom, not in another realm.

Dharma nature is known only in realized wisdom. If you want to know the all-pervading harmony, the peace, and the freedom that cuts through everything, pour your life into the practices that will take us there. Buddhist teachings say that everyone has the capacity to realize wisdom, and they offer a way. There are myriad approaches: meditation and ethical action, the eightfold path, the six paramitas, taking refuge, and so on. As it says in the "Song of the Grass Roof Hermitage," "thousands of words, myriad interpretations are only to free you from obstructions."[34] Here, the exhortation is to believe you can know the Dharma nature and to do what will get you to this realized wisdom, which is simply knowing the harmony, nonduality, peacefulness, and characteristiclessness of every moment.

The *Ten Stages Sutra* is arguably the most influential chapter of the *Avatamsaka Sutra*. It lays out ten stages of development for a bodhisattva: the joyous, the stainless, the light-maker, the radiant intellect, the difficult-to-master, the manifest, the gone afar, the immovable, the good knowledge, and the cloud of doctrine. These are lofty attainments that paint astonishing possibilities. In the Pali Canon the Buddha lays out ever-deepening levels of meditative concentration that lead to "unshakeable deliverance of mind."[35] In the Huayan tradition, where your mind is at right now is the realm you are in. We translate the characters that end this line, 非餘境, "not in another realm," but one could also translate them as "not on another level." That is to say the level of attainment or realized wisdom where one sees Dharma nature is the same as the place where one sees it. Our way of seeing the world is where we are.

This can be seen in the most mundane and the most extreme aspects of human life. Picture a group of small children in the same sandbox, where some are joyously playing, but one is overwhelmed with tears. Both the mutual support and the prejudice and violence that permeate our world are rooted in our ways of seeing. One person might see someone wearing a small round hat and wish them "Shabbat Shalom," while another feels fear and loathing. One person, after being tortured in prison, is shattered for life, while another who experiences similar torments finds inspiration and purpose. Mahayana Buddhism invites us to have compassion for everyone, for all our conditioned ways of seeing, and to practice so we may all be free. The practice of the bodhisattva is unconditional love, of creating the conditions so that no one has to suffer the horrors of torture and incarceration, so no one has to be hated or to hate, so there is no fear of the unknown or the different, so children are listened to and supported when they feel sad. A better world is possible. To practice Buddhism is to create the conditions for people to see the Dharma nature, the wondrous vision of all-pervading harmony of the *Avatamsaka Sutra*. The transformations that Thich Nhat Hanh, Dorothy Day, Martin Luther King Jr., Rumi, Amma, Rabbi Heschel, and the Dalai Lama have brought to the world are not separate from the clarity of their vision of all-pervading love.

Though we practice to create the conditions for well-being, the peace and harmony that this tradition promises are not dependent on conditions. The earliest Buddhist teachings are mostly stories of the Buddha and his disciples. In those stories, when the Buddha awakened he did not find absolute peace by going to a particular place, leaving the suffering world behind, or controlling things. The stories are about him, a human being, traveling in chosen poverty, meeting people who were suffering, and offering them the peace that he had found. His liberation was not dependent on conditions, and it was not in another realm, but he was utterly dedicated to creating the conditions for others to see it.

Implied in this line of our text is the teaching of mind-only, or only knowing. This large body of Buddhist teaching shows that we experience the world only through the lens of our habitual way of experiencing. The *Avatamsaka Sutra* says,

> Of all things seen in the world
> Only mind is the host;
> By grasping forms according to interpretation
> It becomes deluded, not true to reality.[36]

The cutting-through that the last line of the "Song of Dharma Nature" mentioned, and the all-pervading peace of the first lines, are about shedding our interpretations and meeting the world exactly as it is. This cutting-through and this peace are not to be found in another place, another time, or another realm. This is not about escaping from suffering, but about seeing clearly what is right here without objectifying it. Thus, in the Soto Zen tradition in which I am trained, sitting still without trying to accomplish anything or focus on any particular thing; sweeping the floor just to sweep, not to achieve a sweeped floor; listening to someone without trying to fix, judge, or control them—these are both the path and the destination. Whether the tears, the clenched fists, or the laughter are those of ourselves or another, only knowing that it is like this right now has profound power.

In the tenth century, the great Chinese monk Yanshou integrated Huayan, Zen, and Pure Land thought. He wrote, "if one understands the teaching of mind-only, one is able to attain the Path by merely smelling the fragrance of a flower."[37] Outside the bath house at Tassajara Zen Center they have a traditional image of Bhadrapala Bodhisattva entering the bath. In the *Surangama Sutra* he says, "when it was time to bathe, I followed the custom and entered the bathhouse. Suddenly, upon contact with the water, I understood the water was neither washing away the dirt nor washing my body. In the midst of this I became tranquil as I understood there was nothing there."[38] In the direct knowing of the senses, the Dharma nature is known. In the *Blue Cliff Record* we find this version of Bhadrapala's story: "In olden times, there were sixteen Bodhisattvas. When it was time for monks to wash, they filed in to bathe. Suddenly, they awakened to the basis of water."[39] This version of the story teaches that our practice and our liberation is collective. We practice together. Liberation only occurs with the whole world as we meet it with the touch of warm water on the toes, the bracing shock of cold wind down a canyon of city streets, the sound of voices raised in lament, in celebration or in protest, the tang of lemon on the tongue, the shy smile or the inscrutable mask of a stranger passing on the boulevard.

5

True Nature

眞性甚深極微妙

True nature is so very profound, minutely subtle;

I recall sitting in a circle in our third-floor classroom, reviewing a text by one of the founders of Zen. My teacher's method often involved posing questions about a text to see what emerged from the group. In this case he asked, "As the text explains the key differences between meditation and ethical action, what exactly is it saying the differences are?" We puzzled over the thorny text for a while and then arrived at a clear consensus: the text said the two methods are totally different and then describes them in terms that are identical. Because Uisang's poem begins by saying the Dharma nature is nondual, almost every time he makes a distinction he'll also say that the distinction isn't real.

Making distinctions and then seeing that they are not absolute is central to Mahayana Buddhist practice. When I rinse and sort rice, I hope to know that the grit I find and put aside is precious too. I want to understand that different political groups respond to climate change in different ways, but remember that my view of their differences is limited and ever-changing. This enables me to show up for many different ways of caring for our world: fire-breathing oratory about the greed driving ecological destruction, meticulous execution of political strategy, conversation with folks who believe climate change is not caused by human activity, meditative walks focused on the plants and waters around us, arguments about how much to emphasize the disproportionate impact of climate change on people of color, and, just yesterday, bearing witness to acrid haze from fires in Canada obscuring the far shore of the lake across from our Zen center.

The true nature that Uisang introduces in this verse is different from Dharma nature. There are two kinds of nature, true nature and Dharma nature. However, the names sound similar, and their characteristics are similar because they are identical. Guifeng Zongmi, the fifth and last of the great Chinese Huayan masters, was also a renowned Zen teacher. He emphasized their sameness when he wrote, "this true nature is not only the source of the Zen gate. It is also the source of the ten thousand things of the world. Thus, it is also called Dharma nature."[40]

True nature is related to the central Buddhist teaching of dependent origination. Dependent origination means that each thing appears dependent on other things.[41] Dharma nature is related to a Huayan innovation usually translated as "nature origination," which is attributed to Zhiyan.[42] Essentially, nature origination means that things appear dependent on the emptiness, the nirvana, that Buddha sees. Nature origination is the appearance of things that is dependent on nothing; it is unconditioned. If this seems abstract, we can look to the many stories of the Buddha's unconditional compassion and well-being. True nature and Dharma nature are identical because the emptiness of separation that is seen by Buddha is that things appear dependent on other things. However, the distinction between these two natures has practical applications. Because of nature origination, there is Dharma nature, which is incomprehensibly peaceful, complete, and harmonious. Because of dependent origination, there is true nature, which is dynamic and is where we can practice to heal suffering.

The "Song of the Grass Roof Hermitage" says, "the vast, inconceivable source can't be faced or turned away from." The idea that things arise dependent on emptiness, rather than that they are simply empty because they are dependent, could be said to be an innovation or a particular area of emphasis in Huayan. Mahayana philosophy shows that nothing can exist unless it is empty of separate, lasting existence. Huayan teachings point out that this means that all existence depends on emptiness. Being unconditioned is a necessary condition for anything to appear to exist. After these Huayan innovations, we see this theme gain prominence in many East Asian Buddhist traditions, that Dharma nature or emptiness is the "source" of everything. This probably reflects a Chinese impulse to align Buddhist teachings with the indigenous Taoist idea that all clear, distinct things emerge from a dark, mysterious, empty source.

Understanding these two natures makes a vast space of practice out of each moment. I recall giving a talk at a Zen center on the West Coast. I was talking about how ignoring the racist systems we live in perpetuates them, and how seeing that they are an inseparable part of our lives creates a ground for practice. The Dharma nature was there; I had an embodied sense of stillness that pervades everything. I could also see in the subtle changes in the faces and postures of the people in the group, and in my own body, that there were afflictive emotions arising. As the dialogue became heated, I practiced knowing the Dharma nature by noticing the settledness of my body on the earth, intimacy with the people in the room, and the immediate sensations of breath not as a process but as an infinite, still moment. I practiced helping folks there to see Dharma nature, that the peace of the Buddha's liberation was not somewhere else but here in this moment of discomfort and conflict. I practiced knowing and conveying the true nature, that this moment of seeing the anguish that racism has produced is dependent on countless moments of racial harm and the whole web of samsara, and that how we responded in that moment really mattered, for what comes to be depends on what we do.

The characters Uisang uses in this line, which we've translated as "True nature is so very profound, minutely subtle," include a number of connotations. We could translate this line to say that true nature is vast, profound, minute, and subtle. The seminal Soto Zen text "Song of the Jewel Mirror Samadhi" says, "So minute it enters where there is no gap, so vast it transcends dimension." We can see that each thing is dependent on all the things in an entire mountain range, in a single pebble in a mountain creek, in our whole family history, in a face-to-face moment with a sibling, in the vast systems that uphold our culture and economy, and in a gas pump lever squeezed in the hand.

True nature is subtle—it's hard to see, and we miss so much. When we don't see the vast in the tiny and the tiny in the vast, we can get caught. We can be caught in our own attempts to figure things out. My mom told me with a laugh that she thought she had a nice way of living settled at the age of eighty, but lo and behold, the world and her body keep changing. Something new is coming, for true nature is the flux of dependency. As Jin Park writes, "The continued state of tension without ultimate resolution is to be understood as the nature of an entity."[43] As we understand this flux we can also know the Dharma nature and find peace within the changes. The Dharma nature helps us embody trust in the universe, for it is not opposed to anything. The scholar, activist, and Buddhist bell hooks wrote, "trust is the heartbeat of genuine love." We can develop this trust by committing to the simplest of meditation practices, sitting still at dawn day after day and seeing what happens. The body, settled on and part of the earth, can teach our mind to trust. This trust helps us to love, or, as bell hooks put it, "to find ourselves in the other."[44] It helps us to see true nature, to know our utter dependence on each other, and to enact this love, to live for the well-being of everything.

6

It Depends

不守自性隨緣成

Not attached to self nature,
it arises dependent on conditions.

In my early days of Zen practice, I asked my teacher, "I am trying to face my overwhelming shame, rage, and despair. Am I just wallowing in misery or am I being mindful of these emotions in a way that is healing?" He encouraged me to keep practicing with as much kindness as I could and to see that there is no formula, no way to figure it out. I recall walking to the Zen center and opening my senses to the tall green trees along Thirty-Second Avenue as it ends at the shore of Bde Maka Ska, mystified by the pervasive anguish that I could not locate in space, in my body, or in my thoughts. It was clear to me that feelings come from a vast array of conditions, but oh, how I wanted them to be something I could control. I was starting to see the true nature of my emotions, but facing their ungraspability was hard.

Meditation practice can help us to see that thoughts can't be held. Where do they come from? Where do they go? The Huayan ancestor Chengguan wrote, "Since forms come from conditions, they must lack inherent nature or identity. Their lack of inherent nature due to dependence on something else is identical to the completeness of real emptiness."[45] Even a cup of ice water, so vivid, cannot really be held. The sensations, the true nature of what your fingers feel curved around the cool glass, is always and only a momentary manifestation dependent on countless conditions. There is never a return of those particular sensations, and they do not last even for an instant. They are here only in the boundaryless now. That there are lasting distinct and separate entities is an often useful illusion made by the mind. The cool of the glass comes and goes into infinite conditions. Seeing that I can't hold emotions, that they belong to the universe, not me, that they just appear, has transformed my life.

I have met few practices more beneficial than mindfulness of emotions. We can do this at any time. We can turn attention to what has arisen dependent on conditions without trying to fix, judge, or control. We can notice whatever emotion is present, perhaps label it with a word (sadness, calm, anger, shame, bliss), notice whether it relates to any sensations in the body, then bring the attention to whatever seems beneficial to focus on: the breath, the person you are speaking with, the cloth you are ironing, the spreadsheet you are editing, a prayer, or a mantra.

Huayan teachings focus on how things depend on each other, and they focus on why this dependence is wonderful. In general, there is a distinct trend running from the earliest Buddhist teachings, through the Mahayana, to the Huayan, whereby dependency is seen in an ever more positive light. In the Early Buddhist texts of the Pali Canon, suffering and the entire world of samsara arises because of dependent arising. The purpose of practice is to break the chain of conditioned arising and thus to arrive at the unconditioned—that is, nirvana. Later, Mahayana teachings shift from saying the dependent nature of things is the fundamental source of suffering to saying that it is the reason that everything is both samsaric and nirvanic. Because things appear to arise entirely dependent on other things, they are empty of separateness. It is conventional thinking that makes the appearance of conditioned samsaric things, but they are already empty, unconditioned, and nirvanic. The Yogacara teaching of three natures takes a yet more positive turn on dependency. The fact that things are of dependent nature is the middle ground between the imaginary nature of things (samsara) and the complete, realized nature of things, which is blissful, peaceful, and compassionate. This teaching invites us to remain with what has dependently arisen but not grasp at it. This is the way of the bodhisattva: joyful compassion within the conditioned world of suffering. In Huayan, the true (dependent) nature of things is identical with the Dharma (empty) nature. It is replete with everything wonderful that buddhas know and experience. Huayan arrives at the idea that dependency is already complete liberation—and our text hasn't even mentioned suffering!

Suffering is surely real to most people. Huayan teachings focus on helping us see interdependence, because if we do, we will naturally take beneficial action. When Dr. King wrote that we are "caught in an inescapable network of mutuality," he was explaining why he had come to Birmingham to meet violence with nonviolence. Too often, people are spurred to action by feelings that corrode their own well-being: rage, shame, clinging, anger, inadequacy, exhaustion, fear, and so on. I pray that we may create conditions so we may all be free of these. Seeing that the interdependent system we live in can move us to compassionate action, bell hooks wrote, "Our willingness to assume responsibility for the elimination of racism need not be engendered by feelings of guilt, moral responsibility, victimization, or rage."[46] She offers a vision of love in action based on interdependence instead of ideology or afflictive emotion.

The Potawatomi biologist Robin Wall Kimmerer writes, "We are showered every day with gifts, but they are not meant for us to keep. Their life is in their movement, the inhale and the exhale of our shared breath. Our work and our joy is to pass along the gift and to trust that what we put out into the universe will always come back."[47] What we are doing in each moment creates the conditions for what will be. This is a fundamental teaching of Buddhism. The importance of our actions is a subject I explore at length in my two books on Vasubandhu, whom Uisang often cites in his commentary on our text. The ways we perceive and respond to the world are the actions that create our experience. Our cultures, our cities, climate change, international relief efforts, and my mood as I walk to the store—these all emerge as the fruit of countless tiny seeds, moments of action.

Uisang shows a world of wonder, connection, and ungraspability. Imagine what kind of world we make when we see things in this way. As Maya Angelou once said, "You are the sum total of everything you've ever seen, heard, eaten, smelled, been told, forgot—it's all there. Everything influences each of us, and because of that I try to make sure that my experiences are positive."[48] A thousand years ago, the great nun Miazong wrote:

> Killing and bringing to life simultaneously
> The poison and the Dharma nectar together
> Is it a punishment? Is it reward?
> Your guess is as good as mine![49]

Each thing is born in its distinct momentary manifestation right now and is already gone. They are the gifts that shower us. Life and death are right here. Their true nature is dependent on conditions and ungraspable. Miazong does not invite us to figure out whether this moment is something good or not, nor where it came from, nor why it's here. It's here!

In death, the whole world is born. Myriad beings have died. Let us be grateful. Without them and their passing, there is no now for us. As everything you want to grasp disappears moment to moment, what are you bringing to life? What is your offering?

7

Ten Coins

一中一切多中一

Within one is all, within many is one.

If you want to sum up Huayan teachings in a single line, this is as good as it gets. The idea that each thing contains everything and everything is holding each thing pervades the tradition. The implications are vast. When I interviewed folks for an article about Tomoe Katagiri, who was central in transmitting the practice of hand sewing Zen religious garments to North America, Andrea Martin said, "she continually showed that everything matters." If the whole world is here in this cup of tea, this stitch, or this bow, don't you want to care for it? The Huayan master Zhiyan wrote, "because [in the Huayan teaching] phenomena *are* the Teaching, whatever phenomena are brought up, inexhaustible teachings are included."[50] Because everything is precious, discernment about how to care for things is precious. Once, Tomoe was carefully making us tea. Apropos of something we'd been talking about a moment before, I began to quote a line from the *Metta Sutra*. She put down the tea things and faced me with her whole being, relaxed, poised, and alert. When the quote was over, she returned to the tea.

In Uisang's commentary on the poem, he repeatedly refers to the teaching of the ten coins. This is a common Huayan metaphor. If you have ten coins, any one of them completely contains all ten, for if you remove that one, there is no ten. Within the ten coins, each one is completely contained in the ten, for if the ten were gone, so too would be the one. More subtly, if part of the ten were gone, the one would no longer be the exact same one it was. It wouldn't be the one that is thus, in this particular relational context. If a bowl of soup costs ten coins, the one as a part of ten coins is sufficient. As part of nine, it is not.

It is practical for people to agree that one coin always has the same value as one coin, but this is a limited view. A fifty-dollar parking ticket means something very different to someone who is hungry and poor than it does to someone with thousands, millions, or billions in the bank. The power of one coin to buy a cup of tea, or ten coins to buy a bowl of soup, contains the entire universe, which shows up in the form of a mutual agreement between people about the value of a piece of metal. Let us practice looking at money not just in terms of what we have and what we can get, but how this money impacts the whole, and hence, particular individuals within that whole. Our shared agreements about money often hide the fact that within the whole of our economy many individual people work all day for just enough money to live beneath a freeway overpass. These shared agreements can make it seem that someone who doesn't have a job deserves to live under a freeway overpass. Seeing that one is all, we can do better.

The next eight lines of our text will revolve around the theme of "within one is all, within many is one." In his commentary, Uisang says that this and the next line refer to *dharani*. Technically, a *dharani* is a short text that contains or maintains the power or root meaning of the Dharma. It is often a compact summation of a longer teaching. Many sutras have a *dharani* at the end, the chanting of which is understood to hold the impact of the whole sutra. In this case, by *dharani* Uisang basically means teachings. Uisang's point here is that any particular expression of the Dharma contains the whole Dharma, and the whole Dharma upholds or maintains each particular expression. Huayan is explicitly an *ekayana*, one vehicle, tradition, meaning it includes all traditions. Huayan teachings and this line say that all Dharma teachings are included and upheld, not as one monolithic entity, but in their distinctness.

Mushim Patricia Ikeda was trained in a Korean Seon (Zen) tradition and shared this story with me. In the temple they would chant a Hwaeom (Huayan) mantra: HWA OM SONG JUNG. A student asked the teacher, Zen Master Su Bong, "Why are we chanting a Hwaeom mantra? That isn't Zen practice." The teacher chanted "HWA OM SONG JUNG" and said, "How is this not Zen practice?" In one swoop, Su Bong showed that Zen practice means doing what you are doing with your whole being, and that within each Dharma are all Dharmas.

Many Buddhist teachings emphasize one aspect of the Dharma and say that it contains the whole. In the *Mindfulness of Breathing Sutra*, the Buddha teaches that all the fruits of the path can be realized through mindfulness of breath. Many people look to the chanting of NAMU MYOHORENGEKYO, or to the *nenbutsu* (NAMU AMIDABUTSU) as an expression of the whole Buddhist path. Dogen Zenji taught that just to sit zazen is to embody Buddhahood, the entire universe. Mingyur Rinpoche often teaches that each of various Tibetan methods can complete the whole way depending on people's various capacities: analytical meditation, objectless meditation, or chanting and spinning a prayer wheel. Fazang teaches that Huayan practice includes upholding the meticulous precepts of the Early Buddhist schools while also embodying the Mahayana teachings of the *Vimalakirti Sutra* on freedom from conventional ethical norms that can stifle collective liberation.[51] The Dharma lives in surprising places, and a commitment to conventional religious practice can contain some startling freedom. In Japan, Satsujo's parents were concerned that she was too spirited to find a spouse, so they asked her to pray to Kannon (Avalokiteshvara) day and night, which brought her an awakening. "One day her father looked in her room and saw her sitting on a copy of the *Lotus Sutra*. 'What are you doing sitting on this precious scripture?' he shouted.

'How is this wonderful sutra different from my ass?' she replied."[52]

Mahapajapati, the first woman ordained as a Buddhist nun, gave us this poem celebrating her awakening, the sangha, her stepson, Gautama Buddha, and Gautama's mother, Maya, who died in childbirth. She saw that each thing contains the whole, and the whole is whole only because each thing is distinct.

I have been
Mother,
Son,
Father,
Brother,
Grandmother:
Knowing nothing of the truth
I journeyed on.

But I have seen the Blessed One
This is my last body,
And I will not go
From birth to birth
Again

Look at the disciples all together,
Their energy,
Their sincere effort.
This is homage to the Buddhas.

Maya gave birth to Gautama
For the sake of us all
She has driven back the pain
Of the sick and the dying.[53]

Mahapajapati saw that her suffering and the end of her suffering contain a web of lives. She saw that her choice to be a celibate nun, her awakening to an end to birth-and-death, the choice to apply diligent effort to the Way, and the courageous choice of Maya to birth a child in a place where death from childbirth was common—these each uphold and maintain the Dharma, the possibility that we may all find freedom in what Dr. King called our "single garment of destiny."

8

Difference Is Sameness

一卽一切多卽一

One is all, the many are one.

Tibetan Buddhist teachings sometimes invite us to see all beings as our mother. Because of the vast interdependent web of life, at some point in the past each being was once your mother, and hence, should be treated as your mother. Idealizing mothers, and seeing mothers as the natural embodiment of loving-kindness, is a common theme in Buddhist literature. As the *Metta Sutra* says, "Even as a mother protects with her life / Her child, her only child, / So with a boundless heart / Should one cherish all living beings."[54] The idealization of motherhood has various downsides, and some folks have been harmed by their mothers—but as the great Zen nun Miazong said in a startling Dharma dialogue while referring to her genitals, "All the Buddhas of the three worlds, the six patriarchs, and all great monks everywhere come out of this place."[55] To say that, since in the vast web of interdependence every being was once your mother, every being *is now* your mother, aligns deeply with this line of our text: "One is all, the many are one." Not only does one contain all and all contain one, but one *is* all and the many *are* one.

The hallmark of Huayan is to spin wide webs of varied implications of dependency. Huayan texts refer to "Within one is all, within many is one" as the teaching of mutual containment, and "One is all, the many are one" as the teaching of mutual identity. The contemporary Huayan scholar Cheng Chien Bhikshu writes, "Each phenomenon is determining every other phenomenon and is simultaneously being determined by each and every phenomenon. This feature of mutual determinacy, or interdependency, of all phenomena is sometimes translated as mutual identity."[56] Generally, Huayan texts say that mutual containment and mutual identity are both aspects of true nature. They are permutations of the idea that things appear dependent on causes and conditions, rather than being aspects of Dharma nature—in other words, that things appear dependent on emptiness.

Thich Nhat Hanh's poem "Please Call Me by My True Names" brings the teaching of mutual identity into vivid detail. The poem says "I am" a spring bud, a tiny bird, a heartbeat, a victim of brutal violence, their oppressor, and someone who appears to be far from the scene of the horror. For Thich Nhat Hahn, seeing this mutual identity was a call to action, to what he called "engaged Buddhism." Seeing mutual identity does not destroy our differences. It enables us to meet them in a way that is not bound by fixed dualistic views. To love, according to bell hooks, is "to find ourselves in the other." She wrote, "The practice of love offers no place of safety. We risk loss, hurt, pain. We risk being acted upon by forces outside our control."[57] There is actually no way to escape being acted upon by forces outside our control, but we can choose to practice love. We may manifest this love in countless ways: cooking, reading the news, singing, donating money, attending vigils, clearly stating our needs, asking for help, political advocacy, gardening, staying away from someone who harms us, listening deeply, breathing, hugging, watching emotions come and go . . .

When I first came to Buddhist practice, we would sit in meditation before dawn, walk slowly, sit for more meditation as the sun came up, chant the *Heart Sutra*, and then do some cleaning. This remains the heart of my practice. The *Heart Sutra*'s language and message are closely related to the third line of Uisang's poem. I was repulsed, mystified, and eventually challenged by the *Heart Sutra*'s message that there is "no sight, no sound, no smell . . . no mind . . . no path, no attainment, and nothing to attain." The idea that buddhas and bodhisattvas rely on the absence of anything to hold on to—that is, Prajnaparamita—didn't make much sense to me. Eventually, I got into the idea that there is a great peace and possibility in seeing that everything I experience is an illusion created by my patterns of perception, and that ultimately all is an uncontrollable flux beyond names. As I got used to this, I suddenly encountered the opposite message. On a long retreat at Hokyoji Temple I heard the "Sandokai," or in English, the "Harmony of Difference and Sameness," a classic Zen teaching poem that is rooted in Huayan. Right in the middle of the poem we chanted,

> The four elements return to their natures
> just as a child turns to its mother;
> Fire heats, wind moves,
> water wets, earth is solid.
> Eye and sights, ear and sounds,
> nose and smells, tongue and tastes;
> Thus with each and every thing,
> depending on these roots, the leaves spread forth.[58]

I encountered a total affirmation of the immediacy of my senses, of what was right in front of me. This turn from the negative rhetoric of the early Mahayana to the fabulous affirmation of the sensual world is a great gift of the Huayan. We can come to see that the scent of lavender, the sting of sweat in our eyes, the angry face of a colleague on a rough day, or the wagging tail of a passing dog *is* the entire world, the realm where we can practice the fearless love of the bodhisattva.

9

Indra's Net

一微塵中含十方

Within one mote of dust is contained the ten directions.

Chinul is arguably the most influential figure in the history of Korean Buddhism. In the twelfth century, he wrote these lines:

> I came upon the simile about "one dust mote containing thousands of volumes of sutras" in the "Appearance of the Tathagatas" chapter of the *Avatamsaka Sutra*. Later . . . the summation said:
>
> "The wisdom of the Tathagatas is just like this: it is complete in the bodies of all sentient beings. It is merely all these ordinary, foolish people who are not aware of it and do not recognize it."
>
> I put the sutra volume on my head (in reverence) and unwittingly began to weep.[59]

Once, I had just made it through waves of frustration, irritation, and shame while serving as cook for a large group on retreat. As she was leaving, a friend deluged me with appreciation for some brownies I had made on the last day. The drama I experienced while making those brownies seemed so ridiculous. It was such a small thing, yet her appreciation for the gesture was so vast. After I thanked her and she left, I wept salty tears for all of us, at how hard it can seem to simply live and care for each other. This opened the door for cooking at many other retreats with ease, gratitude, and joy.

The "ten directions" are north, east, west, south, northeast, northwest, southeast, southwest, up, and down. A single mote of dust contains all of it. Uisang says the previous two verses technically referred to *dharani*, and how one teaching contains all the teachings. The next few verses refer to phenomena, and how one thing contains all things. Near the end of the *Avatamsaka*, the pilgrim Sudhana tells of what is seen by the many amazing and diverse teachers he has encountered.

In a single atom they see
Congregations, lands, beings, and ages,
As numerous as all atoms,
All there without obstruction.

In the same way
They see in all atoms

Congregations, lands, beings, and ages,
All clearly defined.[60]

An old Buddhist story says Kisagotami was mad with grief as she carried the body of her lifeless baby through town asking for someone to revive them. When she asked the Buddha for help he said she should seek a single mustard seed from a household where no one had lost a loved one. As Kisagotami went from house to house, sharing grief with everyone she met, she realized the completeness of her connection to the web of life-and-death. She thus entered a life of practice.[61]

If we want to see people free from suffering, the way is to fully see suffering. As Cornel West said, "you must let suffering speak, if you want to hear the truth." One tiny moment of sadness, rage, despair, shame, disgust, irritation, or worry contains the entire world. Mindfulness of emotions is one the best medicines we have. When we meditate, we can practice knowing whatever emotions arise without needing to fix, judge, or control them. Throughout the day we can pause, notice the breath in the body, and notice and name however we feel. When we are faced with others we can actively seek to understand how they feel without needing to fix, judge, or control. Because the whole world is present in each ephemeral phenomenon that we call a feeling, each one really matters.

The emotions we experience are part of a vast web of conditions. Contemporary theories regarding trauma are catching up to ideas that have run through Buddhist thought for millennia. The suffering we encounter engenders more and similar kinds of suffering. The suffering we suppress or ignore does not go away. The conditions we collectively create make the moments of experience that make each life, and each tiny action we do impacts the whole. I have walked with Irma Burns, whose son, Jamar Clark, unarmed and Black, was killed by Minneapolis police. I have felt her tears on my cheek, and I have seen her dancing down the street behind a second line band, as the community gathered to stand to support her and the vision of safety for all. Her anguish and her rage are part of a long story of violence, racism, and economic exploitation. Huayan teachings continually point us to the inescapable intimacy of each of our moments to the vast systems we inhabit and co-create. The subtle feeling of lack or need that drives a click on an internet purchase contains the whole of our overheating world. With practice we can learn to see that every moment of feeling is a complete expression of the world, worthy of care and wonder. All the love, resilience, and harms of our ancestors are here, and we are the ancestors of those to come. Let us live like the ones we would love to see in this world.

Gwendolyn Brooks wrote: "We are each other's harvest: we are each other's business: we are each other's magnitude and bond."[62] Bound in interdependence, we are each other's magnitude, our vastness, our completeness. Huayan literature takes up and frequently celebrates an ancient Vedic Indian image, the Jewel Net of Indra. Fazang wrote:

> It is like the net of Indra which is entirely made up of jewels. Due to their brightness and transparence, they reflect each other. In each of the jewels, the images of all the other jewels are [completely] reflected. This is the case with any one of the jewels, and will remain forever so. Now, if we take a jewel in the southwestern direction and examine it, [we can see] that this one jewel can reflect simultaneously the images of all other jewels at once. It is so with the one jewel, and is also so with each of all the others. Since each of the jewels simultaneously reflects the images of all other jewels at once, it follows that this jewel in the southwestern direction also reflects all the images of the jewels in each of the other jewels [at once]. It is so with this jewel, and is also so with all the others. Thus, the images multiply infinitely, and all these multiple infinite images are bright and clear inside this single jewel. The rest of the jewels can be understood in the same manner. If one enters one jewel, one has in fact entered all the layers upon layers of jewels in the ten directions. . . . Thus, while remaining in one jewel, one can

enter all the infinite layers of jewels without actually leaving this one jewel. While remaining in the infinite layers of jewels, one can enter this one jewel without actually departing from these infinite layers of jewels.[63]

10

Infinite Mirror

一切塵中亦如是

Within each phenomenon it is also thus.

A few years ago I visited an exhibition by the artist Yayoi Kusama. There were opportunities to enter several of her "infinity mirror" rooms, small chambers with mirror-lined interiors where little sculptures and lights array with the viewer in an experience of infinitely repeating space. I got into one of four lines approaching the four sides of a box the size of a large wardrobe or a small garden shed. At the front of each line was a person with their face pressed into a small aperture in the box. When it was my turn, I pressed my face into the opening and looked inside. Suddenly I found myself in a vast space filled with glorious multicolored flickering lights. My face and the faces of three other people I had never seen were a couple of feet apart and repeating in kaleidoscopic relationships out to the far reaches of the horizon of my ability to see. Intimacy and awe swept over me. "My" reflected face was no different than the faces of the three other people peering into the box, the many reflected faces, the lights, the flickering, the space itself. Then someone stuck a phone into the face port. We were phones! The shattering of the intimacy of faces so close for the hope of capturing infinity in a photograph was so poignant, and yet nothing was broken. The space remained space, and I stepped aside to let someone else have a turn.

* * * * *

Empress Wu is widely considered the only female sovereign in the history of China. She was closely associated with Huayan and drew authority from claiming the power of the *Avatamsaka Sutra*'s main icon, Vairocana Buddha. I do not think theocratic government is a good idea. However, there is something inspiring in the fact that this singular matriarchal figure drew authority from these particular teachings. This authority was surely related not only to the many powerful female teachers in the final chapter of the *Avatamsaka*, but also to the Huayan idea that each part contains the whole.

Fazang was the empress's teacher. He was looking for a way to convey the interdependence and nonobstruction that define Huayan. He built a small room whose walls were all mirrors, placed a lamp and a Buddha statue inside, and entered with the empress. In the endless reflections she realized the vastness of their relationship. After they had some time to get accustomed to the spaciousness, Fazang held out a small crystal ball. They looked inside the tiny reflective object and saw the entire space of repeating buddhas, selves, and light in the palm of his hand.[64]

The Huayan traditions emerged from many streams, but one of the earliest texts that became incorporated into the *Avatamsaka Sutra* is the *Purifying Practice Sutra*. It is composed of about 150 verses, and each one is an invitation to see the thing or the activity right in front of you as an opportunity to meet the world with the aspiration that everyone be free from suffering. You can find several of these verses in the introduction to this book. The fact that every phenomenon contains all phenomena emerges from *Purifying Practice*'s calls to humility and care in daily life. Dorothy Day was instrumental in founding the Catholic Workers Movement, which brings aid to the poor while engaging in nonviolent direct action to end the systems that create poverty. She wrote, "We must lay one brick at a time, take one step at a time, we can be responsible only for the one action of the present moment, but we can beg for an increase of love in our hearts that will vitalize and transform all our individual actions."[65]

The *Avatamsaka* says bodhisattvas, "knew sentient beings are empty and have no existence, but did not deny the fruits of action."[66] The philosophical basis on which we say that each being is full of the whole universe is that each thing is empty of separateness. Neither this completeness nor this emptiness removes the central Buddhist teaching that what you do matters. Uisang focuses on seeing the wonder, beauty, and benefit of interdependence. It is also good to keep in mind that there is an awful lot of suffering, and we can do something about it. The Yogacara Buddhist teachings of Vasubandhu that inform Huayan are much more explicit and detailed in this regard, and Uisang refers to these at numerous points in his commentary on the text. Yogacara teachings emphasize that each thing we do plants seeds that create the conditions for our shared world. The way we think, feel, perceive, act, and speak all come from conditions and go into further conditions. This is a description of karma—that is, "action" and its fruits. Yogacara teachings help open the door to the full implications of Huayan; our karma not only accrues to individuals moving through samsara lifetime after lifetime, but also provides an explanation for why what we do matters for all, and why liberation for everyone is possible. Each action has an impact, and each impact contains everything.

Generally speaking, the Huayan tradition focuses less on karmic processes than the Yogacara does. The Yogacara approach invites us to observe and transform the intentional quality of our actions. Huayan teachings focus on seeing what is in front of us as so precious that we naturally act in a way that is compassionate and liberating. In a seminal Huayan text, Fazang teaches that each atom contains everything, and then goes on to teach that if we know this then we will practice four virtues.[67]

The first virtue is responding to each moment with compassion unfettered by conventional norms. We see this reflected in the startling behavior of Zen teachers. In the old stories, Zen teachers shout to wake up their students, elevate an illiterate woodcutter insulted as a "jungle rat" to the highest rank, and support women as leaders in defiance of patriarchal norms. One teacher even decides to die standing on his head. In our current lives there are plenty of harmful conventions that we can challenge with compassion. We can crack through old behaviors that exclude some people from our Buddhist communities, that push queer folks into closets, that have given us exclusively male U.S. presidents, and that create an economy that strips our mother earth for our daily conveniences. We can also challenge Buddhist conventions that allow teachers to cause harm by saying that they are beyond conventional ethics.

The second virtue is "maintaining dignified, well-regulated, exemplary conduct." Fazang explains this as meticulously following conventional ethical norms. This is an essential antidote for the tendency to go too far with the first virtue.

The third virtue is "treating beings gently and harmoniously, honestly and straightforwardly."

The fourth is "accepting suffering in place of all sentient beings. This means . . . practice—not for one's own sake, but wishing generally to benefit myriad beings." We can take care of ourselves and each other in ways that are truly wholesome. As an addict, I thought intoxication was my only medicine. As a recovering addict, I've learned a few things. Taking care of myself in ways that don't benefit the whole isn't actually taking care of myself. Taking care of others in ways that leave my well-being out is not truly for the benefit of all.

11

Time and Timelessness

無量遠劫卽一念

Immeasurable distant eons are one moment of mind;

Fazang brought Empress Wu into the mirrored hall, full of an infinite regress of reflections of the lamp, the Buddha, the empress, and Fazang himself. They saw the tiny and the vast, the particular and the universal, integrated before their eyes. At the end of the presentation, Fazang said that although he had found this way to show that one is all and many is one, he couldn't find a simple way to show that this is true of not just things, but also of times. It's hard to *see* that every moment is all time, and all time is in this moment.[68]

In Huayan it is essential to know that when these teachings speak of a particle of dust, or a phenomenon, they are talking about a particular momentary experience. When Fazang teaches that a house is entirely dependent on a single rafter, he's not referring to an abstract rafter or house; he means this exact house and rafter at this exact moment.

Sure, you can replace a rafter, but you will not have the exact same house. All of time only and always shows up for us in the form of particular moments. Nothing is left out of the web of causes and conditions. Zhiyan wrote, "It is like the various interdependent elements of a house. . . . If we explain cause and result by the comprehensive [Huayan] school, we introduce remote causal factors into the near; therefore when the house is complete everything is produced at once. If there is a single thing that is not established, this house is not established either. It is like this: if the first step arrives, all steps arrive. If the first step does not arrive, then all steps do not arrive."[69] If this moment can only be possible within immeasurable distant eons exactly as they were, how can we say they are different things? Being not different, they are identical.

Fazang wrote, "Because an instant has no essence, it penetrates the eternal, and because the lengthy epochs have no essence, they are fully contained in a single instant. . . . Therefore, in an instant of thought all elements of the three periods of time—past, present, and future—are fully revealed."[70] Moments don't have boundaries. Can you find the beginning or the end of this moment? This is worth investigating with some meditative attention. Is there anything in any moment that is entirely fixed and unchanging that you can actually grasp? Perhaps try holding a teacup to see if the perceptual experience of the teacup remains identical for any time whatsoever. Ideas of continuity that seem quite absolute are momentary impressions, which are themselves in flux, even though they seem lasting. Certainly, just because something seems fixed and lasting does not mean that it is. In his seminal essay "Uji" (Being-time), Dogen wrote, "Things do not hinder one another, just as moments do not hinder one another."[71] Can the last moment get in the way of this one?

There are revolutions in perception when folks see that things we once thought of as lasting, distinct phenomena are relational processes. Scientists see that mountains, ravines, prairies, and species of birds, grasses, and primates are constantly in a state of transformation. This view gives us the modern sciences of geology and natural selection. Arguably the general direction of science has been to see that what appear to be fixed things are relationships and processes. Copernicus opened people to the idea that the heavens don't revolve around the earth, and later we found that even the sun is hurtling through space. Now we have general relativity, where time, space, and gravity fold together, and quantum physics, whose relational implications are still unfolding.

The Huayan view of time permeates the teachings of Dogen, who uses many literary devices to help us let go of a linear view of time where objects last and bump up against each other. He points to two liberative views. There are ungraspable moments of experience, which he calls "dharma positions" or "phenomenal expressions," and there is a total interrelationship of all time and space. In his essay "Genjokoan" he writes, "Firewood becomes ash, and it does not become firewood again. Yet, do not suppose that the ash is future and the firewood past. You should understand that firewood abides in the phenomenal expression of firewood, which fully includes past and future and is independent of past and future."[72] The utter preciousness of each moment is revealed in the appearance of firewood disappearing, simultaneous with the appearance of heat, smoke, ash, and everything everywhere—that firewood exists utterly alone only in the very moment of its vanishing, that is, its union with the whole. The firewood is gone even as it is revealed by the processes of unknowable distant time.

William Faulkner wrote, "The past is never dead. It's not even past."[73] His work looked into the hearts of a vast web of people living in the legacies of enslavement, Indigenous genocide, family trauma, and economic exploitation. James Baldwin disagreed bitterly with Faulkner's admonitions to go slow in the work for racial equality, but they shared something of the Huayan vision of time. Baldwin wrote, "The great force of history comes from the fact that we carry it within us, are unconsciously controlled by it in many ways, and history is literally present in all that we do."[74] These teachings are an invitation to see that all the love and all the harm of this world is here in our lives. Buddhist teachings say we can look into the ways we see the world, formed, as Buddha taught, by karma without discoverable beginning. So rather than repeating the same old patterns, we can act for liberation. Mindfulness is about seeing the processes that create suffering; ethics is about bodies creating freedom from suffering. Knowing the totality of our connection, the immense limits of our ways of knowing, and our mere "moments of mind," we can make an offering for the well-being of all. Dogen wrote, "The time-being of all beings throughout the world in water and on land, is just the actualization of your complete effort right now. Closely examine this flowing; without your complete effort right now, nothing would be actualized, nothing would flow."[75]

12

This Really Matters

一念卽是無量劫

One moment of mind is immeasurable eons.

"One moment of mind" here refers to what in Sanskrit is called a *citta*. In this context it has two basic meanings. Technically it refers to a particular aspect of momentary experience of mind: sadness, joy, energy, an ache in the foot, a word being heard or appearing as a thought, the perception that a patch of color is green, or that the patch of green color is a leaf, and so on. Or it can refer to the entirety of a moment of experience: all the sights, sounds, emotions, smells, bodily sensations, thoughts, and tastes taken as a whole.

There is a tendency in Buddhist teachings to speak of things not as absolutely existing objects that are observed, but as direct experiences. The commitment to mindfulness of the body that pervades Buddhist thought is not about objectifying and manipulating the body, but rather it is about becoming deeply intimate with the experience of the body itself. Each sensation in the body—for example, the warmth of a hand on one's palm, the coolness of an ice cube on the tongue, an ache behind the eyes—each of these is a citta, a moment of experience, a moment of mind. We can't experience the past, we can't experience the future, and we can't experience anything outside of what we are experiencing now, this moment of mind. In the Yogacara traditions, which in East Asia became known as the Mind-Only school, there are extensive proofs and investigations into the idea that everything we experience is merely mind.

"The triple world is mind only." One could easily argue that this is the most famous line in the *Avatamsaka Sutra*. It appears in many variations in East Asian Buddhist literature. Technically, the sutra says that bodhisattvas at the sixth stage "realize the three realms are only mind."[76] The three realms here refers to places one can live and states one can experience through meditation: the desire realm, the subtle-materiality realm, and the immaterial realm. The main point of this quotation is to say that whether one is a dog, a pig, a snake, a gardener, a salesperson, a student, a late-stage Alzheimer's patient, a yogi dwelling in utterly blissful meditation, a fourth-stage bodhisattva, a god, or a ghost, you are experiencing the world as you are experiencing it. Processes of mind, that is to say karma, such as emotion, thinking, perception, and bodily actions, are creating the conditions for the realms where we will live. Ultimately, the point is that what you experience is the result of actions, and what you do creates what will be experienced.

This moment of mind, your moment, is as vast as all time, for it contains everything and is also in the process of creation with everything. Rigoberto Menchu is a K'iche' Guatemalan Nobel Peace Prize laureate who has poured her life into work for Indigenous people. She once said, "I am like a drop of water on a rock. After drip, drip, dripping in the same place, I begin to leave my mark, and I leave my mark in many people's hearts."[77] Just as modern geology formed from the perception that mountains and oceans are made by processes as small as grains of silt being carried by drops of water, so too we can see that human flourishing, and the flourishing of all our plant and animal kin, are here in our most tiny actions.

Dogen founded the Soto school with teachings deeply embedded in the idea that each moment is intimate with all time. Knowing this, the practice of the school is to care for what is right here. The practice of zazen is often taught in terms of meticulous attention to posture. Walking meditation involves precise attention to lifting the heel as one inhales and placing the foot as one exhales. Dogen is at his most inspired when he describes the practice of cooks at Zen temples—people lovingly attending to the rice, the greens, and the fire. As he ends his essay "Tenzo Kyokun" (Instructions to the Cook), he refers to the importance of cultivating three kinds of mind. He offers these instructions for those who are caring for the food in the kitchen at Zen temples, but also as instructions for anyone caring for any aspect of the world.

First, he exhorts us to find "joyful mind." This is the joy that comes from being grateful that we can serve. No matter how poor the materials at hand or how rough the circumstances are, you have an offering of value. Second, he invites us to find "kind mind." He says this is the mind of a parent; sometimes folks like to call this grandmotherly mind. This is about deeply caring about those around you and offering your energy to their well-being. Lastly, he calls us to "great mind." This is the mind that does not discriminate, a vast space where everything that happens can occur without disturbing us. Uisang says the mind is already great, for every moment of mind includes all time! We can, though, aspire to realize this, and we can create the conditions for a world of joyful, kind, and great mind.

Realizing our interdependence with all time can be scary. We may want to shy away. Dolores Huerta, a founder of the United Farm Workers Association, once said, "We criticize and separate ourselves from the process. We've got to jump right in with both feet."[78] Hers was a call to face the historical conditions of exploitation with nonviolence right now. But that can be difficult, as bell hooks wrote, "When we face pain in relationships our first response is often to sever bonds rather than to maintain commitment."[79] Huayan teachings invite us to see that we cannot actually separate ourselves from the process, but we can choose how to engage. We will not heal the harms of the climate crisis by pretending that we are not part of the crisis, nor can we end the pervasive inequity in the world by ignoring it. Our moments are bound to it all. Objectifying and avoiding don't actually feel good or help. Meeting violence with nonviolence, arousing joyful, kind, and great mind, dripping, dripping like water on a rock, we are a part of mountains meeting the sea.

13

House and Rafter

九世十世互相卽

The nine times and the ten times are mutually identical,

When Uisang traveled to China for the Dharma, he met a woman named Seonmyo who fell in love with him. He told her that his vow of celibacy meant he could not requite her love, and her ardor to protect him on his path transformed her into a dragon. After years of caring for him on his travels she became a great stone hovering over invaders outside one of the first temples he founded. She is perched there now, a great stone guardian overlooking the Temple of the Floating Stone, Buseoksa, near Yeongju City in Korea. The times of myth, of history, and of the present can collapse in a good tale.[80]

Trauma, too, can make the interpenetration of times vivid. Yesterday someone described being overwhelmed by emotions during an argument with a friend. Suddenly, they had the jarring experience of being a three-year-old child feeling the same rage, the same need to hold someone at bay who won't say no, that was showing up in their present life. This collapsing of time and identity rang true to my own experience when I was receiving treatment for posttraumatic stress. Somehow, I could be totally aware of my own bodily sensations, my own present-moment sensory environment, my own agency and adulthood, and also absolutely *be* the terrified child consumed by shame, terror, and rage—a child who in linear time had grown up thirty years ago.

Teachings on karma have much in common with contemporary theories of trauma.[81] So does the Huayan emphasis on the interpenetration of past, present, and future. Scientific data show the deep relationship between a child struggling to find food and safety in an impoverished neighborhood and an adult being pushed into a prison cell. Understanding karma can help us know the importance of our actions. Knowing interdependence opens up space for compassion and shows that we can create conditions for freedom for everyone.

Many Buddhist texts refer to the three times: past, present, and future. Characteristically, Huayan literature expands this list to ten. The *Avatamsaka Sutra* states that bodhisattvas have ten ways of speaking of the past, present, and future: the past, present, and future of the past, the past, present, and future of the present, the past, present, and future of the future, and the past, present, and future all being one instant of the present.[82] So the nine times are the past, present, and future of the past, present, and future.

The tenth time is all time being in a single moment. Regarding the tenth time, Pobyung writes, "If one does not look toward the before and after, contains them summarily, and severs the opposition, then it becomes the tenth time period of the characteristic of the whole."[83] His language recalls the third line of our text: if we cut through all distinctions, this moment is the whole deal. Past, present, and future are ideas, not things. Or as Albert Einstein once said, "time and space are modes by which we think and not conditions in which we live."[84]

This verse is telling us that however you slice time up, all the parts are identical. When making this kind of claim, Huayan teachers often refer to the six characteristics: whole/part, sameness/difference, and integration/disintegration. This pervasive Huayan teaching is based on Vasubandhu's commentary on the "Ten Stages" chapter of the *Avatamsaka*.[85] It is articulated in one of the most well-known Huayan teachings, Fayan's teaching on the house and the rafter.[86] Here the house represents the whole, and the rafter is a part. Without the rafter there is no house. Sure, as I wrote in a previous chapter, you can have a different house that doesn't have this rafter, but it won't be this particular (whole) house. The house we are talking about in this verse is all of time: past, present, and future. If any one of its rafters—that is to say moments—is missing, then it isn't this exact whole. Can you remove any moment from eternity?

Early Buddhist teachings help us to see the parts rather than a unitary self. They provide mindfulness methods so we can shift from thinking, "I am angry," to being aware of the parts that make up this apparent anger: a thumping heart, muscle tension, racing thoughts, and an angry feeling. Mahayana practices help us let go of the dividing mind, so that instead of thinking "I am angry," we are instead aware of the whole nondual field of our experience, where there is no object toward which we can direct anger. We see the whole rather than the parts. Fazang points to the seamless integration of these two sides of the coin. A penny needs the side with Abe Lincoln on it, and the Lincoln side depends on the whole penny.

Thus we move to the next two characteristics, sameness and difference. Fazang says the rafter is identical to the house. Since the whole entirely depends on the rafter and vice versa, they are identical, the same. In order to see the rafter as different from the house, you need to be thinking of the rafter as something that can be removed or separated from the house, and it can't be. If it were removed, there would be a different house and a different rafter. That different house and different rafter are imaginary, in that they are not the whole and parts that are here right now.

Here's another way to think of the sameness of things that appear to be different. All the characteristics we ascribe to things that make them different are not absolutely real. This is the subject of the third line of our text: "Without name, without characteristic, cutting through all." If everything that makes two things different is gone, we are left with sameness.

If the hull of a ship is gone, is the ship there? What identity does the ship have without the hull? How much of the hull has to be gone or present for it to be the ship? Any claim that there is an exact point where a part ceases to be identical to the whole is ultimately arbitrary. Surely, I can imagine a me without feet, without facial hair, without a body, without emotions, without the thoughts that are here right now, or without a heartbeat, but those imagined "mes" are ideas; they are not the actual whole that is here. The parts cannot be absolutely separated out, and thus they are identical to the whole. On the other hand, the parts have to be different parts or the whole wouldn't exist. The *Avatamsaka Sutra* repeatedly describes worlds and people living inside the pores of the skin of the Buddha. The reason we are identical to Buddha is that we are different. There can be no sameness without difference. My body and its parts are identical because there are different distinct parts.

On to the last pair of characteristics: integration and disintegration. The rafters, the studs, the foundation of the house all must be integrated to make the house, but the distinct character and function of each part is not destroyed, and also remains utterly unique, unintegrated. When you dance a couple's dance, you are integrated, a function of the dance, but you are still a separate nonintegrated part—just you functioning in your own way! Each moment functions within the whole of time but is also unmoving, not integrated, utterly unique. Audre Lorde saw practical implications of this view when she wrote, "Without community, there is no liberation . . . but community must not mean a shedding of our differences, nor the pathetic pretense that these differences do not exist."[87]

Things come together and they come apart. Come on over and take this rafter from my house to build a raft, and maybe it will get us to the other shore. The integration of the conditions of my life and their disintegration are inseparably bound. In birth is death. In something entirely new, the old is both destroyed and not destroyed. Holding this view, I can see that trying to cling to anything is a ticket to angst. All of time is integrated right here and disintegrates right here too. There may be pain as we touch this truth—but oh, there is also a vast space of liberation, the freedom to act for the liberation of all beings throughout space and time right now.

In ritual we can embody the collapsing of the nine times, and the ten times. Years ago, I was kneeling in the basement at our Zen center chanting the three refuges in Pali. My baritone voice filled the cement block room, so tiny in the vastness of time. I felt, as I chanted the very words that Buddhists have intoned to enter the Way for twenty-five hundred years, that the voice was not mine, but the voice of ages, not of my body, but of countless bodies, of a young woman near the Ganges in the fading evening light, going for refuge. There I was, exactly me. Just as now, you are absolutely you.

14

All Alone

仍不雜亂隔別成

Yet not mixed or disordered, they arise separately.

In Zen practice we often stand with hands in *shashu*, the left above the navel with the thumb tucked into a fist and the right hand embracing the left. Zhiyan wrote, "It is like the five fingers making a fist, but not losing fingerhood: though the ten time frames are simultaneous, yet the ten time frames are not lost."[88] With hands in shashu we attend to this moment, but all time comes together in this simple embodiment. We practice together in a room, one body, these many bodies, my own body. We can practice feeling each finger, and the whole hand.

This verse echoes the *Avatamsaka Sutra*: "In this ocean of worlds / Are inconceivably many world systems, / Each one independent, / They are not all mixed up."[89] Each moment of experience, each moment of mind, is its own crystalline, unique jewel, set within the linear order of time and the many other cosmic orders of the universe.

Uchiyama Roshi wrote, "Time exists for us because we compare one moment with another, and in the welter of perception we feel time flowing swiftly."[90] You may recall that I saw Pomnyun Sunim demonstrate the relative nature by showing that a tall flower was only tall when compared to a shorter one. First he held up two flowers and asked us to say which one was tall, then he held up a single flower and asked whether it was tall. In a brief moment of not comparing it to anything else, I saw the stark aloneness of that single flower. This is something that seems to arise for folks in meditation practice, a sense of the utter *thisness* of something we encounter. Eventually we may learn the Buddhist terms of art: *thusness*, *suchness*, *tathata*, *dharmata*, *tattvartha*. For all times to be identical, they need to be utterly distinct—otherwise, they would be neither the whole nor the parts that they actually are.

Buddhist meditation practices often produce these two senses of time: a feeling of profound connection to the past and the future, and a sense of the startling, contained aloneness of this moment. What is actually alone is the moment of mind, of experience, not the person apparently inside it. Sometimes this is not evident and folks find a bleak sense of isolation within this moment, standing alone with nothing to compare to, nowhere to go, nothing to accomplish, to fix, to gain. If we persevere, we can find that we are not alone in the moment. The sights, sounds, thoughts, bodily sensations, emotions, impulses, smells, and tastes all arrive together, complete. It's not a matter of a self arriving to observe some stuff, but of a moment arising, with some little part of it perhaps seeming like an observing self. Even so, no one else can ever be in this exact moment as it is for you. Uchiyama Roshi wrote,

> The first-person "I" is totally my own life experience; it is separate from everyone else's. It is from that viewpoint that my teacher Sawaki Roshi pointed out that there is no way I can share even as much as a fart with another person. And yet, everyone living out their life as they experience it, as wholly theirs, is simultaneously the eternal, or universal aspect of self. The self is not universal in an abstract sense; it is so in a most concrete way. There is nothing abstract about all human beings living out one and the same fresh, original life force. There can't be anything more concrete than that.[91]

Let us care for our hearts as we move closer to the completeness of each moment. We may be overwhelmed by the vastness of our connection to the suffering world, our tiny stature under the aspect of all time, or our utter apparent distinctness. Where we find sorrow or fear, we can meet it with compassion; where there is joy and energy, we can let it flow. The Chan nun Chaoyan wrote,

Above the highest peak of Mount Wu, the round moon is alone,
Cold and bland, pure and poor, it doesn't possess a single thing.
If someone should come along and ask what this nun is doing.
She sits for long hours on her meditation mat enjoying herself.[92]

Seeing the aloneness of this moment and its total connection to all times can disarm our attempts to control things, to wait for liberation. They can open us to seeing the utter preciousness of this opportunity to live and act from a vow that all beings be free. We can be free to act without frustration of our desires, for there is not some future to control, some past to repair. Our fixed views about ourselves and others can't be absolutely true, since this moment is always totally distinct. Still, it is so easy to hold on to them: "that guy is a jerk"; "it's hopeless"; "we must win"; "trying to stop this pipeline didn't work so there's no point in trying"; "she is perfect"; "Zen is the one true Way"; "I don't like gardening."

You may love gardening, but I tend to not enjoy gardening. I have learned, though, that not liking gardening is a unique experience every time. I try to enjoy it! There are moments in the garden where I have forgotten to have a bad time. I can enjoy those too. There are not these lasting things somehow separately dragging themselves through time. There are only distinct moments interbeing with the whole, and there is always and only process and relationship.

15

The Awakening Heart

初發心時便正覺

The mind's first aspiration for awakening is true awakening.

This line is a direct quotation from the *Avatamsaka Sutra*.[93] It refers to the central Mahayana Buddhist concept of *bodhicitta*, awakening mind. A person who aspires to awaken so that everyone can awaken has tasted "the mind's first aspiration for awakening." At some point a person may realize they want to give their life so that everyone may be liberated from suffering. Rosa Parks said it well: "I would like to be remembered as someone who wanted to be free . . . so other people would be also free." Many Buddhist traditions extol the wonder and power of bodhicitta. They provide ritual, meditative, and teaching contexts to awaken our hearts to this compassionate aspiration. In the "Ten Stages" chapter of the *Avatamsaka Sutra*, there are ten distinct steps on the path to true awakening, complete buddhahood, starting with an initial moment of bodhicitta.

However, the description of each stage seems to contain every liberative quality one could possibly imagine.

All the previous verses about time point in one direction: an utter lack of limitations on our aspiration to care for people. Uisang cites the *Srimaladevi Sutra* in his commentary. In the sutra, Queen Srimala preaches the teachings of the *tathagata garbha*, the womb of Buddha, also known as buddha nature. This is the inherent capacity for and state of liberation of all sentient beings. She says, "Because, Lord, the Tathāgata does not dwell within the limits of time; the Tathāgata-Arhat-Samyaksambuddhas dwell at the uttermost limit. The Tathāgatas do not have a time limit for their compassion or for their pledge to heal the world."[94] Although the views of time in Huayan texts have interesting parallels to contemporary scientific and metaphysical views, their point is that we are called to a compassion that is utterly limitless. Speaking of the bodhisattva's vow to liberate all beings, the *Avatamsaka Sutra* states, "As long as earth exists / As long as all beings exist / As long as acts and afflictions exist / So long will my vow remain."[95]

In Soto Zen we value bodhicitta but don't talk much about attaining enlightenment. We deemphasize attaining something else and focus on practice now, on this moment of aspiration as true awakening. At the end of most of our services we chant these bodhisattva vows. We focus on the activity of making the vows together, not on individually attaining the immeasurable aspirations they point toward.

Beings are numberless, vowing to free them
Delusions are inexhaustible, vowing to extinguish them
Dharma gates are boundless, vowing to enter them
Buddha's way is unsurpassable, vowing to become it.

A few months ago we had a nun from China, Venerable Ding, stay at our Zen center for a month. At the end of her stay she gave a talk. She said, "please raise your hand if you aspire to attain enlightenment in this lifetime." In stunned attention almost everyone sat still. Then she said, "I aspire to attain enlightenment in this lifetime." She too was talking about bodhicitta.

Chinul teaches that first we attain an initial awakening experience, then we practice to deepen it. The *Ten Stages Sutra* and Chinul's exhortation to attain awakening so you can practice both point to something evident in the stories of the Buddha. *Buddha*, which means "awakened one," devoted his life to living simply, being at peace, and helping other people be well in ways that were flexible and responsive. The endpoint of the path is just the path. This is so evident in the teachings of the "Gandavyuha" chapter of the *Avatamsaka*. The little pilgrim, Sudhana, carried along by bodhicitta, never stops opening to new relationships and teachers. The teachers show many ways. Their various realizations are practices: feeding people, providing medicine, guiding folks through storms, freeing prisoners, healing with touch, and teaching Dharma and mathematics. The twenty-fifth teacher that Sudhana encounters,

Vasumitra, helps folks to meet their sexuality without repression, harm, or affliction.[96] Nothing is left out.

The *Mahayanasamgraha* refers to the six paramitas as the "cause and result" of understanding. It says they are cultivated through "faith in the teachings, . . . relishing, rejoicing, and delighting."[97] The six paramitas are generosity, ethics, endurance, energy, concentration, and wisdom. These form the path of practice in the Mahayana, and in the *Avatamsaka*, four paramitas are added, filling out the auspicious number ten: skillful means, aspiration, spiritual power, and knowledge. These are both the cause and the result of awakening. In one sutta from the Pali Canon, the Buddha teaches that the path leading to nirvana is mindfulness of body, and is "the destination and the path leading to the destination."[98] All these teachings collapse the difference between your moment of practice now and the total liberation from suffering that Buddhism promises is possible.

In the final pages of the *Avatamsaka*, the buddha of future birth, Maitreya, extols the power of Sudhana's aspiration for enlightenment for all. He says just as one lamp can light a million lamps without being diminished, so too can one aspiration for awakening light millions of aspirations.[99] I remember sitting across a table at a coffee shop with a fellow recovering alcoholic. He'd been clean for a few weeks—a great achievement in my mind. I'd been sober for a few years. He was speaking of a brokenness, a gaping chasm between himself and the life he wanted, the person he wanted to be. I saw him with the eyes of all who had sat with me, heard with the ears of hundreds of people who sat in circles and listened to my own story of brokenness, of waiting to be free. This hearing didn't see the gap. This seeing heard nothing broken. We were together, complete. We cared enough, had compassion enough, to meet on the path, guided perhaps by just a spark from a flint, or maybe a blazing sun of aspiration for well-being.

16

Samsara and Nirvana Are Not Two

生死涅槃常共和

Life-and-death and nirvana are always identical;

The start of the path and the completion of the path are not separate. Every overwhelming or barely noticeable moment of suffering that arrives in samsara—that arrives because things come to be and pass away—is inseparable from the cessation of all suffering, from nirvana.

In chapter 8, I addressed the overall Huayan logic for why each distinct thing is identical to each other distinct thing, and here this thinking is applied to samsara and nirvana. Although this may seem abstract, in his commentary on this line, Pobyung writes: "Samsara is precisely your body and nirvana is precisely your body."[100] Everything is right here.

Last week I was sitting with my back to a slab of granite overlooking a lake in the Rocky Mountains. I had a couple hours of rest in the midst of leading a weeklong wilderness meditation retreat. Sound carries far over water, and I could hear folks climbing the mountain above me and others fishing down below. I could see quiet retreatants across a bay basking on the sun-hot rocks and swimming in the icy turquoise water. The sensations of the body were deep and settled, the boundary between the warm stone and skin indistinct. All the voices, the words, and the hearing were suspended in the broad field of sound, sight, sensation, thought, and smell. There was no escape from the aches of the body, the shouts of the climbers, the frustration of a fisher, her line tangled in brush, the ground squirrels whistling warnings as an eagle passed above, the knowledge that this resting would end and cooking pots and the rocky trail would call us onward. There was peace.

Fazang wrote, "Because sentient beings are deluded, they think illusion is to be abandoned and think reality is to be entered; when they are enlightened, illusion itself is reality—there is no other reality besides to enter."[101] When Buddha realized nirvana, he did not stop seeing loss, grief, death in childbirth, illness, aging, or any of the anguish that comes with them. He was in nirvana, a state of not wanting and not pushing away, right in their midst. He visited the dying, he counseled the bereft, he faced an army preparing for battle. He met them with compassion and with total confidence that each person could attain the nirvana that he saw right in life-and-death. Dogen wrote, "those who have great realization of delusion are buddhas; those who are greatly deluded about realization are sentient beings."[102] Things seem to come to be and pass away, and the causes of our suffering seem so absolute, but we can be aware that everything we think is a thing is not a thing. Mind makes us see a world of objects coming and going, but this is a profoundly limited view. Nirvana is not the destruction of apparent objects; it is seeing that those objects aren't absolutely real, so we don't have to suffer from our fixed views—and we don't have to cause suffering based on those fixed views. The great Chan teacher Yun Men taught, "Medicine and disease subdue each other: the whole earth is medicine, what is your self?"[103]

The fact that this moment of awareness has arisen is bound to the process of your dying, to the raw physicality of your mother giving you birth, to all the patterns of harm that have ever been: the wars, the famines, the exploitation, the cruelty, the loved ones lost, the swearing over stubbed toes, the irritability with friends, the cruel internal dialogues, the food binges, the stinging eyes full of sweat, the pains in our once-young bodies. It's all here, and when we open up to the whole of it, let go of the part-making views, and smell what's here, feel it, see it, we might forget that we need to argue with the universe. We might feel that the whole earth is medicine. We can realize that our self is doing something right now from a place of connection, of compassion, of care, without needing to figure it out.

17

The Fourfold Dharma Realm

理事冥然無分別

Universal and particulars are thus unfathomable, not distinct.

The fourfold dharma realm, or four *dharmadhatu,* is one of the most influential teachings of the Huayan school. This teaching explores the relationships between the universal (理, *li*) and particular (事, *shi*). Like many Huayan teachings, these four can sometimes seem like a ring of ball bearings in constant motion, where distinctions are made and immediately erased. They provide practice for flowing through the friction caused by fixed views. Garma Chang writes, "The wider and more vague the connotations of a word are, the more useful that word might be for Hwa Yen. To Hwa Yen a word is quite useless if it is not flexible and inclusive. . . . Li, in different contexts, can mean, 'principle,' 'reason,' 'universal truth,' 'the abstract,' the 'law,' 'noumenon,' 'judgment,' 'knowledge,' and so forth. Shi can mean a 'thing,' an 'event,' a 'particular,' the 'concrete,' 'phenomenon,' 'matter,' and so on."[104]

The *universal* here basically refers to the emptiness of anything that appears to be a thing, and it has the two universal qualities of not lasting and not being separate. *Particulars* here has a complex array of meanings: things, affairs, phenomena, dharmas. Many Mahayana teachings investigate the relationship between emptiness and dharmas. Here *dharma* refers to an experiential event, a phenomenon, as opposed to *Dharma*, meaning truth or teaching. These are dharmas: a scent, the naming of the scent "lavender," the positive feeling that arises in relation to that scent, the desire to bring it home. . . . The term *shi*, or particulars, carries the meaning of *dharma*, but also of things and affairs. It connotes something a little more solid and real than a dharma. A monk asked Dongshan, "What is Buddha?" and he answered, "Three pounds of flax."[105] Dongshan didn't analyze his experience as a set of dharmas: a visual percept, the naming of the material (flax), the emotion associated with it, and the mind's inclination to measure (three pounds). He addresses it in its conventional apparent thingness; he addresses the state of affairs. You are asking about Buddha. I am weighing flax. This distinction may seem subtle but many scholars point to the tendency of East Asian Buddhisms to shift from the Indian emphasis on analyzing mental processes to an emphasis on taking care of affairs and things. This shift is embedded in Dongshan's teaching and in the idea of *shi*, particulars, that we find in this line.

The Huayan teaching of the four dharma realms originates in a text called the "Mirror of Mysteries of the Universe of Huayan" by Dushun and Chengguan.[106] These four realms are (1) particulars, (2) the universal, (3) the nonobstruction of universal and particulars, and (4) the nonobstruction of particulars and particulars. Each of these realms is where we are. When we see things as things, we are in the realm of particulars. When we see things as empty, we are in the realm of the universal. No matter how we are seeing things, we are also always in all four realms.

The Huayan teaching of four dharmadhatu was carried forward in Chan schools. The terms *host* and *guest*, *darkness* and *light*, *trunk* and *branches*, *absolute* and *relative* are frequently used in both Huayan and Chan teachings to explore concepts like the universal and particulars. The Linji (Rinzai) school includes a teaching called the "fourfold host and guest," and the Caodong (Soto) school expanded on the four with a teaching called the "five ranks." These all expand on the relationship between universal and particulars laid out in Huayan dharmadhatu teachings. The classic Soto Zen liturgical text "Harmony of Difference and Sameness" invokes the four dharmadhatu with the lines "Phenomena exist; box and lid fit. / principle responds; arrow points meet."[107] The "Song of the Grass Roof Hermitage" keeps its reference simple: "although the hut is small it includes the dharma realm."[108]

The first dharma realm is particulars and the second is the universal. The third dharma realm is the one referred to in this line of Uisang's text: "Universal and particulars are thus unfathomable, not distinct." The nonobstruction of the universal and particulars is often expressed in Mahayana literature in this line from the *Heart Sutra*: "Form is emptiness, emptiness is form." All forms—that is, sensory experiences—are empty of lasting, separate nature. On the other hand, there must be form for there to be emptiness. For something to be empty of lasting separate nature, it has to be a thing. Nothing can't be green, and nothing can't be empty. This may seem like word games, but this teaching says that universal and particulars do not obstruct each other. If you think that seeing that things are empty means they don't matter, then you are caught on the idea that emptiness obstructs things. If you think that well-being depends on things, then you are caught by the idea that things obstruct emptiness. The fact that there is nothing that lasts to hold on to, and all the distinctions our minds make are not absolute truths, does not obstruct that fact that we have the capacity to take care of what is happening, what is here.

The fourth dharma realm is one of the distinct innovations of Huayan thought: the nonobstruction of *shi* and *shi*. Things do not obstruct things. Seeing the third dharma realm allows us to respond to apparent objects without believing we can control them. Seeing the fourth dharma realm invites us to fully engage with all the particular things as they operate harmoniously.

A common metaphor says the host is universal and guests are particulars. The host is a space, an emptiness, where things are welcomed. Since universal and particulars are identical, then each particular is also a host, welcoming all guests within. Since all particulars are hosts, they mutually contain each other.

Chengguan explains particulars, universals (noumena), and then the logic by which he claims particulars do not obstruct other particulars: "phenomena basically obstruct each other, being different in size and so forth; noumenon basically includes everything, like space, without obstruction: merging phenomena by noumenon, the totality of phenomena is like noumenon—even a mote of dust or a hair has the capacity of including the totality."[109] If form is emptiness, then a kitten is empty, a cloud is empty, and the cloud and kitten are both empty. Since the kitten and the cloud are empty, they do not obstruct, completely contain, and are identical to one another. All this while licking their fur and gliding through the sky in their completely distinct ways. When disaster comes to others, if we know they are ourselves, compassion flows. When we are judging and shaming ourselves and we realize we are every other person, we may find a little more kindness. When Thich Nhat Hanh wrote (in his poem "Call Me by My True Names") "I am" a bird, a flower, the victim of brutality, the perpetrator, and the witness, it was a call to action, to practice.

Zen student Myo-On Hagler neared the end of a row of stitches. This last row marked the end of many challenging months of sewing the robes that symbolized her ordination as a Soto Zen priest. She paused in the silence that prevails during sewing practice, thick with devotion and mindfulness. Needle poised above the last stitch, she asked her teacher, Tomoe Katagiri, "Is there anything to be said for the final stitch?" Tomoe said, "The last stitch is the same as the first."[110]

Chengguan wrote, "What embraces the myriad things is the mind, and the mind, once merged with the myriad things, is the four Dharma-realms."[111] The teaching of the four dharmadhatu is about our actual experience; it does not occur somewhere else or speculate about things beyond our knowing. In the tenth century, the Korean monk Kyunyo Sunim commented on this line in Uisang's text referring repeatedly to "visualization."[112] You can imagine the four dharma realms, and you can also see them.

When the "Mirror of Mysteries" introduces these teachings it is in the context of teaching us how to cultivate meditation. The text refers to cessation and contemplation. You may know these by various near synonyms: samatha and vipassana, or concentration and mindfulness.[113] Dushun invites us to contemplate the second, third, and fourth dharma realms in sequence: contemplate emptiness, contemplate that form is emptiness, and finally contemplate "universality and inclusion."[114] The details of the means of contemplation in the text are beyond the scope of this book, but I invite you to open to the possibility that through commitment to meditation practice and to contemplating these teachings, you may see the ungraspability of things, embody the compassion that comes from meeting each ungraspable thing with your whole heart, and know the boundless harmony and joy that comes from seeing that everything is included in each thing.

18

Awakening and Action

十佛普賢大人境

This is the realm of the ten buddhas
and Samantabhadra, the great ones.

This verse is about the relationship between compassionate action and awakeness. Although hundreds of bodhisattvas are named in the *Avatamsaka Sutra*, it is particularly associated with Samantabhadra, the bodhisattva Universal Good. This being is known for compassionate action and, as it says in the *Avatamsaka*, the "the immense pure energy of the joy of universal good."[115] Often depicted riding a white elephant and generally understood to be male, Samantabhadra figures sometimes have feminine characteristics, similar to Guanyin, the bodhisattva of compassion.

In the final pages of the sutra, Sudhana, having met and learned from teachers who serve people in so many ways, merges with Samantabhadra. They recite a set of verses that close the text. Here are some excerpts, the first of which may be familiar to some as a part of daily Soto Zen ritual.

Whatever evil I may commit
Under the sway of passion, hatred, or folly,
Bodily, verbally, or mentally,
I confess it all.

And whatever the virtue of beings everywhere,
Hearers, saints, self-conquerors,
Enlightening beings and buddhas,
In all that I do rejoice.[116]

. . . .

I will traverse the paths of the world
Free from compulsion, affliction, and delusion,
Like a lotus unstained by water,
Like the sun and moon unattached in the sky.

Extinguishing all the miseries of bad states
And bringing all beings to happiness,
I will act for the welfare of all beings
In all lands everywhere.[117]

. . . .

May there be no limits to practice,
And no limit to virtues;
Persisting in infinite practices,
I know all their miraculous creations.

As long as the earth exists,
As long as all beings exist,
As long as acts and afflictions exist,
So long will my vow remain.[118]

This final collection of verses in the sutra have been chanted for fifteen hundred years to evoke the power of the vow to free everyone from suffering. When you see someone you deeply admire who pours their energy into caring for people, for animals, for the soil, the air, or the waters, when I stand in solidarity with Indigenous water protectors here on Dakota land, I remember that this effort has impact, and it comes from causes and conditions. We are creating the world we live in, and the world to come. We are the fruit of seeds, and we are planting seeds. Let us cultivate the joy of universal good.

Zhiyan wrote, "'Cause' means cultivation of appropriate techniques, investigating with the whole body, and fulfilling all the stages [of enlightenment]. This is what is represented by the bodhisattva Samantabhadra. The 'result' means the complete result of ultimate dispassion and extinction of own-being, the realm of ten Buddhas, where one is identical to all."[119] The appropriate techniques presented in the last chapter of the *Avatamsaka* are so varied: meditation, listening to Dharma talks, offering food, creating medicine, crafting beautiful perfumes and fabrics, pilgrimage, studying grammar, healing touch, erotic contact, challenging the authority of kings, complete self-sacrifice, enjoying the fragrance of flowers and the chime of bells. In each case the focus is on doing the activity with compassion and wisdom: caring deeply for how people are and understanding what will actually help everyone be free from attachment. These actions are the cause of awakening, of *bodhi*. Practical methods of creating beauty and ending violence, ignorance, and deprivation are essential to the Mahayana path of collective liberation.

Uisang's commentary on the "Song of Dharma Nature" describes the ten buddhas. "The first is the buddha of non-attachment because he peacefully abides in the mundane world and achieves complete enlightenment. The second is the buddha of vows because he has been born [in order to liberate living beings]. The third is the buddha of karmic rewards because he has faith. The fourth is the buddha of maintenance because he obediently follows. The fifth is the buddha of transformation because he everlastingly ferries [living beings to the other shore]. The sixth is the buddha of the dharma realm because he pervades everything. The seventh is the buddha of the mind because he peacefully abides. The eighth is the buddha of samādhi because he has no limits and no attachments. The ninth is the buddha of the nature because he is determined. The tenth is the buddha of wish fulfillment because he universally covers everything."[120]

Uisang invokes a joyful bodhisattva who is known for harnessing the power of an elephant to help people and thus causes an array of ten buddhas to appear. The text says,

"This is the realm of the ten buddhas and Samantabhadra." How did we get to this realm? How did you and I end up in the wondrous realm where such compassionate, wise beings have awakened from suffering and are acting for our welfare? Huayan teachings remind us that the most wonderful things we can possibly imagine are already here, and we can learn to see them. The *Avatamsaka* says, "The Buddha body responds to all—none do not see it."[121] The great Indian Yogacarin Dignaga wrote, "It is the naturally pure cognition of ordinary beings that is expressed by the term 'buddha.'"[122] What you are experiencing right now can't be separate from all the buddhas and the compassionate action of Samantabhadra because *buddha* refers to the fact that nothing in your field of experience is separate in the ways it seems to be. To be awake is to be awake. The question is, what will we do with this moment of awakening?

The buddha most associated with Huayan and the *Avatamsaka* is Vairocana. Sometimes known as the pure *dharmakaya*, this is the Dharma body that knows no separation. Although emptiness is inseparable from form, and Buddha can only appear as particular people and things, it's still empty: ungraspable, all-pervasive, and beyond conceptual limitations. I found a stone statue of Vairocana at the Smithsonian museum. The entire standing Buddha figure is covered in tiny carved images depicting the complete array of things in our universe and beyond. The whole world is the body of Vairocana, and the body of Vairocana is the whole world.

When you look into your body, everything is there, and when you act with the body, you are acting with the whole world. Pobyung wrote, "Introversion is precisely Ten Buddhas and extroversion is precisely Samantabhadra."[123] These teachings point to a balance between meditation and action. It helps to find some clarity sitting in meditation so we can embody the bodhisattva way when we stand back up. Embodying the bodhisattva way in daily life is also the cause of meditation. Although ultimately there is no separation, it helps to find our balance between these two. The "Song of the Grass Roof Hermitage" says "Turn around the light to shine within, then just return."[124] In meditation we can slow down and know the sensations in the body and the emotion that is here, then open up to sight, sound, thought, smell, taste, and touch. In action, we can speak with kindness, directness, and truth. We can cook food, organize a food drive, listen to our children, edit documents, hang laundry on a line, show up at vigils, smile at clerks, vote, speak our minds, give things away, give money away, give our effort away. We can let effort and ease flow from our vows, our aspirations for everyone to be free from suffering.

19

The Ocean Mirror Mind

能仁海印三昧中

In the midst of Buddha's Ocean Seal Samadhi,

Uisang's Seal of the Huayan One Vehicle Dharma Realm is sometimes known as the Ocean Seal Chart. It is a map and a stamp. It describes the Ocean Mirror meditation, which itself bears the seal of authentic awakening. Being "In the midst of Buddha's Ocean Seal Samadhi" refers to times when we settle into clear awareness, and also to the idea that right now we are located in the Buddha's all-inclusive awareness. Fazang wrote, "The so-called 'Ocean Mirror' [is a metaphor that] symbolizes the innate Buddha Mind. When [the manifold] delusions are exhausted within, the mind will become serene, limpid, [and unruffled], and the infinite reflections of all phenomena will appear at one time. This may be compared to the stirring up of ocean waves when the wind blows; and their subsidence when it stops, leaving a calm and pellucid surface where all reflections may be clearly seen."[125] This is a state where we can see all the sufferings of the world without adding a single drop. Referring to the dusty world of suffering, the Chan nun Zhitong wrote:

> Within the vast expanse of dust, essentially a single
> suchness.
> Whether vertical or horizontal, everything bears the
> seal of Vairocana.
> Although the entire wave is made of water, the wave is
> not the water.
> Although all of the water may turn into waves, the
> water is still itself.[126]

Pobyung writes "'Ocean Seal' is an absorption on the storehouse of purity."[127] The Yogacara teachings on the storehouse consciousness deeply influenced Huayan. In early Yogacara teachings, this storehouse, the root consciousness or *alayavijnana* is the unconscious process whereby our actions plant seeds for what we will experience and where those seeds bear fruit. Our experience is the fruit of previous seeds. This process is the cause of suffering and also the reason our actions matter. It is possible to overturn the root, or transform the basis of this process, so that we don't suffer and don't cause suffering. As Yogacara teachings developed in China, especially in the *Lankavatara Sutra*, the storehouse consciousness is given a much more positive light. Since all things are nirvanic in nature, the teachings began to emphasize the essentially liberated nature of this root consciousness, or as Pobyung says, its purity. It becomes identified with buddha nature: the inherent state of Buddhahood and the capacity to attain Buddhahood. The relationship between this uncontaminated basis of awareness, on the one hand, and the passing afflictions of our lives, on the other, can be compared to the relationship between water and waves.

The cessation of suffering that constitutes the third of Buddha's Four Noble Truths is described in the *Awakening of Faith*, a central text of first-millennium Chinese Buddhism. "What we speak of as 'cessation' is the cessation of the marks of the [deluded] mind only, and not the cessation of its essence. It is like the case of the wind that, following the surface of the water, leaves the marks of its movement. If the water should cease to be, then the marks of the wind would be nullified and the wind would have no support [on which to display its movement]. But since the water does not cease to be, the marks of the wind may continue. Because only the wind ceases, the marks of its movement cease accordingly. This is not the cessation of water. So it is with ignorance; on the ground of the essence of Mind there is movement. If the essence of Mind were to cease, then people would be nullified and they would have no support. But since the essence does not cease to be, the mind may continue."[128]

This passage tells us that nirvana is not nothingness. The emptiness of realization is not nothing, but rather, it is that experience is empty of the causes of suffering. I have had the great fortune to spend a lot of time on meditation retreats in the mountains gazing at crystalline lakes. I have seen the breeze move slow ruffles across their soft surfaces; I have seen loud, clashing waves spray and spill over one another onto rocky shorelines; and just last week, I saw stars reflected in the deep unmoving blackness of still water. So too with practice, through all kinds of winds and waves, we may realize a stillness unbroken by stars, sirens, storms, irritation, schedules, desire, racing thoughts, fear, or stillness itself.

In Dogen's essay "Ocean Seal Samadhi," he writes, "All of the Buddhas and Ancestors invariably enter the meditative state that bears the seal of the Ocean. As They swim about in this meditative state, there are times when They give expression to the Truth, and times when They experience the Truth directly, and times when They put It into Their daily practice."[129] We can find this clear awareness in meditation and we can bring it to the world. The *Avatamsaka Sutra* says:

> The ocean has a special extraordinary quality—
> It can be an equal reflector of all,
> Sentient beings, precious things, rivers and streams—
> All it contains, prohibiting none.[130]

When Jamar Clark was killed by police in Minneapolis in 2015, I began attending events led by Black folks who, like me, want to end police brutality and racism. I do my best to bring the Ocean Mirror, to be completely present to the people there: the anguish, the rage, the strategizing, the varying views, the joys, the connections, the chanting, the mutual support. Around that same time I was invited to provide mindfulness training for some police departments. Listening to police officers, I heard stress, tension, camaraderie, relief, and resistance. I helped us find inclusive, compassionate awareness—one of the most powerful tools we have for ending harm. I try to share the Ocean Mirror: the compassion, the care, the space, the spaciousness. With police and in the streets, I sometimes see my own anger, frustration, and despair with the ongoing suffering, and I try to make space for them all.

Outside the third precinct station in Minneapolis, a few days after the murder of George Floyd and the day protestors burned it down, I walked slowly in the robes of a Buddhist priest. I heard the chants, the roars, the tense lulls in the crowds of thousands, the intermittent thud of helicopter rotors, inhaled the acrid smoke of a burning car, the tear gas fired by the police, their pepper spray, saw a middle-aged Black woman tackle a white male teenager throwing rocks at police, heard Marvin Gaye, Aretha Franklin, Kendrick Lamar, saw a circle of American Indian Movement folks form around someone to protect him, saw a crowd of citizens facing a crowd of heavily armed and armored police emerging from military vehicles and between them a line of middle-aged Black men standing hand in hand as the police deployed a cloud of tear gas, a roaring crowd of youth arriving atop a battered pickup truck, my own sadness and exhaustion, and my own inescapable connection to us all.

20

The Wish-Fulfilling Jewel

繁出如意不思議

The abundant manifestations of wish fulfillment are inconceivable.

The wish-fulfilling *mani* jewel has been a part of Buddhist literature from the earliest times. Pali sutras say a wheel-turning king will have a mani jewel to benefit the people. In Prajnaparamita literature, the jewel is medicine that permeates things with its beautiful colored radiance. The first Yogacara text, the *Samdhinirmocana Sutra*, says that everything is of complete, realized nature, like a jewel that reflects characteristics based on how we view it, but is adamantine, empty, and flawless beyond all our projections. Mahamudra texts say the mind is like a jewel where manifestations appear in its empty luminosity. Indra's Net, the pervasive Huayan teaching, is a net of jewels. Dogen wrote a gorgeous essay called "One Bright Pearl," and the *Avatamsaka Sutra* includes the word *jewel* thousands of times.

Here in Buddha's Ocean Seal Samadhi, the manifestations of the wish-fulfilling jewel are inconceivable. We cannot possibly comprehend all the wonderful results of the vows of bodhisattvas. In each moment, we receive a world replete with the results of the hopes of past generations that we may be free from suffering. Our ancestors' dreams for us are alive in each moment if we look, if we realize the mirror, the ocean that is our mind, our experience: the sights, sounds, smells, tastes, bodily sensations, thoughts, and emotions. This teaching is to evoke a sense of abundance. It is to cut through anxiety, alienation, and clinging. Early Buddhist texts focus on giving things up so we can be free of our clinging. Huayan emphasizes seeing a world so replete with riches that we feel no need to hold on.

Huayan teachers understand that these abundant manifestations require our actual giving. In his commentary on this line, Pobyung writes, "It may be compared to the wish-fulfilling [gem] possessed by a wheel-turning king [*cakravartin*]. If it is kept in the royal treasury, it does not rain down all manner of treasures."[131] In a Pali Canon text, a king gets wise counsel on how to deal with bandits overrunning the realm. His adviser tells him that punishment and violence will not end the epidemic of crime. But, "with this plan you can completely eliminate the plague. To those in the kingdom who are engaged in cultivating crops and raising cattle, let Your Majesty distribute grain and fodder; to those in trade, give capital; to those in government service, assign proper living wages. Then those people, being intent on their own occupations, will not harm the kingdom. Your Majesty's revenues will be great; the land will be tranquil and not be beset by thieves; and the people, with joy in their hearts, playing with their children, will dwell in open houses."[132]

This sutta is reflected in the final chapter of the *Avatamsaka*. A young seeker named Jewel Light tells Sudhana about meeting a king who has made giving and nonviolence his way of governing. When she meets him, this king has laid out a great mass of goods to give away. Seeing this, she takes off her jewelry and adds it to the offerings. Then she sings many verses celebrating the king's practice. Here are a few:

> For many years there was no rain . . .
>
> The rivers all went dry, the parks were like deserts;
> Before you appeared clear-eyed, the earth was strewn with bleached bones.
>
> Now you have joined with the needy, and all are satisfied—
> Coming forth, you shower gifts on the four quarters, fulfilling all, low and high.
>
> There are no more thieves, mercenaries, or frauds—no one is killed or injured;
> None go hopelessly to death . . .[133]

Once, after a visit to a juvenile detention center to provide meditation instruction, I called my mother, who taught art in a similar facility. I was talking about how bleak the environment was. She said, "for a lot of my kids, this is the safest place they have ever been." This stung, but it rang true. I know we can do better for folks who do harm, which includes all of us. Punishment does not lead to greater well-being. When people have a propensity for doing harm, I believe we should limit their ability to do it again, but I pray that we may create ways to promote public safety that are about providing people the resources they need to be well, which fundamentally includes being of benefit. Does our well of genuine resources really run dry? Do we need to hoard compassion, food, medicine, and shelter?

In the *Avatamsaka*, one of the teachers whom Sudhana meets is a lay woman named Prabhuta. She says, "I have attained an enlightening liberation which is an inexhaustible treasury of manifestations of good. From this one vessel I satisfy sentient beings of various tastes with food conforming to their wishes, with various sauces and spices, of various colors and aromas. From this one vessel I satisfy even a hundred beings with whatever food they wish, even a thousand beings, a hundred thousand, a million, a billion. I satisfy untold numbers of sentient beings of various tastes with whatever food they wish, gratifying and pleasing them and making them happy—and yet this vessel does not diminish or run out."[134]

I am aware that no one around here has a pot that produces infinite food, but if we cultivate the mind that says abundance comes from giving, what might happen? It is inconceivable how much effort, care, and giving parents provide to children every day. Sure, sometimes we get exhausted, frustrated, burned-out, clingy, or caught by parental martyrdom, but every day the well of giving that naturally emerges from parents is mind-boggling. The capacity of human beings to manifest boundaryless, unattached giving is not a myth or a fairy tale. It is natural and common.

Sudhana meets an earth goddess. She and her companions emerge from the earth with an array of wonders.

> All the leafy trees simultaneously produced new growth, all the flowering trees blossomed in unison, and the fruits of all the fruit trees became fully ripened. All the rivers wove together their flowing currents and all the lakes and ponds rose to abundant fullness.
>
> A fine rain of perfume fell, everywhere soaking the ground, whereupon a breeze arose and scattered blossoms everywhere across it as countless musical phrasings simultaneously resounded and all the heavenly adornments emanated exquisite sounds. . . .
>
> Sthāvarā, the earth spirit, then placed her foot on the earth, whereupon hundreds of

> thousands of . . . jewel treasuries spontaneously welled up and emerged from the earth. She then told Sudhana:
>
>> Son of Good Family, these jewel treasuries that have now appeared here follow along after you. They are the karmic fruition of the roots of goodness you planted in the distant past that have been drawn forth by the power of your karmic merit. You should freely put them to use however you wish.[135]

Sudhana, called ever onward by bodhicitta, by care for the well-being of everyone and everything, sees vast powerful reserves of energy and support pouring from the earth, beautiful and awesome. He knows that he can give it all away. The fruit of his practice is this magnificent moment and an opportunity to see what's next.

21

Seeing the Rain of Jewels

雨寶益生滿虛空

This rain of jewels benefits all life, filling all space.

A few weeks ago, my brother stepped into the cabin where we were staying with our mother and invited us to look at a moose he'd just seen in a nearby lake. When we arrived, there were many folks on the shore looking, but the moose had left, annoyed by all the onlookers. We sat as an evening squall blew in over the towering cliffs of the continental divide to the west. In the shelter of a pine, we watched the droplets pelt the water, mesmerized as patterns of rippling circles intersected and disappeared. The sun burst through above the divide as the clouds flowed east, and as the rain poured into the thirsty earth, the rays of the sun turned the air into a field of glittering gems. Drops flashed and glinted and disappeared in the space of the sky and the space of the lake.

The *Avatamsaka* says, "The Buddha, in every single instant / everywhere showers the boundless rain of truth."[136] This truth is that we are not subjects and objects, but total intimacy. In *Braiding Sweetgrass*, Robin Wall Kimmerer mourns the fact that her students believe that the human relationship to the earth is inescapably extractive and harmful. She shows ways that Indigenous folks view the earth and act in a way that is mutually supportive. People and land can care for each other. She writes, "Paying attention is a form of reciprocity with the living world, receiving the gifts with open eyes and open heart."[137] Karma teaches that what we do, how we view the world, and the quality of intention we offer are what create the experiences we have and the world we live in. What if we realize that nature and humans are not separate things? Just as oaks and black-eyed Susans drink the water from the sky then give it back, so do you and I. The path of destruction and exploitation that has been part of human life for oh so long is not destiny. Buddhist teachings are clear: we have a choice, and what we do matters. The earth goddess gave Sudhana the jewels to use. How will you and I meet this boundless Dharma rain?

This rain of jewels fills all of space. Everything that appears is empty, and thus full of the radiant sustaining goodness of Buddha. If everything is empty of separateness, and liberation from suffering is merely knowing this, how can it not be so? Dogen opens his most central essay thus: "As all things are Buddhadharma, there is delusion and realization, practice, and birth and death, and there are Buddhas and sentient beings."[138] These teachings say the truth is not somewhere else; it is available in this very moment.

Many Mahayana teachings say the truth is right here, but we may not know we are seeing it. Seeing the truth from a Buddhist perspective means seeing in a way that is free from suffering and from the causes of suffering. It means knowing what to do that will be of benefit, and doing it. I know people often don't see a world of abundance and goodness. I cling, I judge, and I push away—and I'm not alone in this regard. The Four Noble Truths don't explain why suffering arises and then just tell us to stop doing it. They give us an eightfold path of practice that leads to the truth, the boundless healing rain of Dharma, the end of suffering. The paramitas, which we explored earlier in the chapter "An Awakening Heart," offer a path of practice in the Mahayana that is both the way and the destination. Addiction, violence, and abuse are personal, but they are also completely collective grounds for suffering. No one act, and no one person, will end the path of environmental devastation we are on. None of us can end transphobia, antisemitism, trauma, Islamophobia, or racism alone. But what we do matters. The Buddha awakened, and then he stayed awake for the world. If we give ourselves to practice for liberation, we may sometimes see the Dharma rain, and we may see it in unique ways. We may find the beauty in the path, so fraught with the anguish of samsara. The Chan nun Zukui left us a verse:

The yellow elm tree at the corner of the house
Has stood there for who knows how many years.
This morning the winds whipped up a storm,
Leaving the ground strewn with coins of gold.[139]

22

Skillful Means

眾生隨器得利益

All beings benefit according to their capacities.

Imagine a panic in a crowded theater. Everyone believes there is a raging fire. People are trampled in the fight for the exits. One person knows there is no fire; they know who shouted *fire* and why. Trying to explain to people over their cries and curses that there is no fire will not help in this desperate flight. A wise one lifts folks up so they are not trampled and helps us all move safely from the peril of our terror. *Upaya*, skillful means, refers to the ability to tailor our liberative actions to the needs of the current moment and the people we are with. It is esteemed throughout Buddhist literature, and in Huayan texts is included as the seventh of ten paramitas.

The benefit that this line of text says we receive is the ability to act in a way that ends suffering. We receive the capacity for upaya. Each one of us arises from causes and conditions. This is our true nature. It is not fixed. It is not, as the sixth line of our text says, "attached to self-nature." The benefits of the Dharma rain come to us only in the way we are conditioned to receive them, and they come differently moment to moment. Many of my friends, after numerous trips to addiction rehab, finally receive the truth that they don't have to keep on with the same anguish and can walk a path of recovery. So many seeds of compassion had to be planted before most people in the United States came to believe that Jim Crow was a horror and a crime. Buddhist women have been advocating for equal status and access for thousands of years, and I pray we may today be ready to receive their wisdom.

In an early Huayan text, Dushun writes: "Prescriptions are designed in response to illness; when the illness is ended, the prescription is finished with. Medicine is dispensed to quell attachments; when attachments are gone, the medicine is done with. Since illnesses are manifold, the medicines given are not one. According to potentials, progress and practice differ; therefore techniques are not the same."[140]

Myo-O Habermas-Scher told me of a meeting with her teacher, Katagiri Roshi, when she was utterly bereft after losing her first child, the day after he was born. She asked, "Why are we alive?" Katagiri said, "'Why?' is already extra." She cracked open to the immediacy of her anguish, to a vast compassion. The power of this direct teaching came from the trust they shared. It came from the teacher's knowing of the student's capacity to face the fact that her attempts to explain her loss were a way of avoiding the truth of her grief. If someone comes to you with this question, though, I do not recommend repeating his answer. When people grieve they need food, healing touch, and deep listening. In the final chapter of the *Avatamsaka*, the laywomen Prabhuta and Vasumitra and the great bodhisattva Avalokiteshvara give these to the suffering as their teachings.

In the final pages of the *Avatamsaka*, Sudhana enters a tower that contains infinite other towers, each with an entire universe inside. In the pages that describe what he sees there, it says, "He saw countless enlightening beings on the promenades or sitting on their seats engaged in various activities. Some were walking around, some were doing spiritual exercises, some were practicing observation, some were projecting universal compassion, some were working on various sciences having to do with the welfare of the world, some were instructing, some were reciting, some were writing, some were asking questions, some were engaged in ripening conduct, concentration, and knowledge, some were undertaking vows."[141] Then Sudhana bowed with his whole body in all directions.

Let us learn to trust that everyone has their own unique capacities. We can learn to bow to them all. Flowers, hungry children in a shantytown, squirrels, people practicing law, folks raised to believe that being gay brings divine punishment, roofers, magpies, people who were hale all their lives suddenly beset by a crippling chronic illness . . . The conditions that form who we are in any moment are incredibly various. So too are the things we have to offer. This teaching, and all Buddhist teachings, say that no matter what, we do have something to offer. We can take a step on a path of freedom from suffering.

A friend told me his recovery sponsor once said, "If God wanted it done perfectly, he wouldn't have sent either one of us." I am completely ignorant about God, but what is clear to me is that I don't know the whole story. I can't know, be, or grasp some perfection. When we realize that we benefit according to our capacities, we can be free of trying to figure out what's right, and be free to do our best right now.

As Chinese teachers studied the array of texts coming from India, they were faced with contradictory teachings: meditation must involve analysis or it must not, realization is gradual or sudden, the mind is fundamentally pure or impure, and so on. Huayan calls itself a one-vehicle tradition, *ekayana*. The Huayan tendency was to include all the teachings, but to classify them in terms of stages of understanding. These classification systems are known in Chinese as *panjiao*. Rather than focusing on how one teaching is wrong and the other right, they instead emphasized that certain teachings were appropriate for certain kinds of people. However, they also tended to say that there is a progression, and certain teachings point more directly to the truth. Not surprisingly, Huayan teachers put the Huayan teaching at the apex. Different teachers created different hierarchies, but in general they tended to put the Pali Canon teachings at the bottom, differing Mahayana teachings—such as emptiness, mind-only, buddha nature, and the Zen teaching of sudden awakening—in various orders, and then place Huayan at the top, as including them all.

I often find myself facing the challenge of trying to be as inclusive and respectful of people's differences as possible, while also being ready to speak up for what I believe to be most beneficial. As I work to create multifaith communities, sometimes my respect for difference rubs rough against my calls to dismantle inequities based on gender and sexual orientation. It is clear to me that I do not have and will not find a solution. I have capacities arriving at this moment to meet others with their own capacities, and a precious chance to make an offering. I have found that the work of letting go of harm—whether it be from discrimination, addiction, abuse, trauma, or exploitation—is most powerful when it is rooted in authentic relationships. I try to recall the path of humble encounters walked by the little pilgrim Sudhana. If I start out telling people they are wrong, or only gather with folks who agree with me, I often miss the opportunity to deepen the trust that creates our most powerful shared capacities.

23

Practice Being Home

是故行者還本際

Thus the practitioner returns to the true source.

It is practice that brings us to realization. Practice means what you are doing and what creates our future experiences. When you practice a scale on the piano, you play the scale, and you create the skillful playing of future scales. Teachings on karma emphasize that what we do now plants the seeds for the lives we will have in the future. James Baldwin, seeing so much suffering in the world, said, "People pay for what they do, and still more, for what they allow themselves to become, and they pay for it very simply; by the lives they lead."[142] This reflects the classic Buddhist view of karma and samsara. Our Huayan text, of course, emphasizes the positive. With practice each person can arrive where they already are, which is the source of all existence and all liberation.

The term *benji* (本際) at the end of this line carries a complex array of meanings: true source, reality limit, boundary of realization, primordial realm. Essentially it is synonymous with "reality" or Dharma nature. The Dharma nature that Uisang describes in the opening of this poem is closely related to the idea of nature arising; all phenomena depend on emptiness, the truth that Buddha sees. Buddha—awakened, unconditioned awareness—is the source of everything.

Uisang here reminds us that although we are already in reality, with practice, we can know it. We can find the freedom, the compassion, and the blissfulness of being awake. This reminder comes after several lines pointing out that we all have our particular conditioned ways of being. This line says, "*Thus* the practitioner returns to the true source." It is through our practice as people with various habits and backgrounds that we can come to the truth that Buddha sees. It is because we are limited and conditioned that we can return to the limitless, unconditioned present moment.

In his commentary on this line, Pobyung writes, "Because these practitioners know that one's own body and mind are precisely the essence of Vairocana, it is called 'returning to the original source.'"[143] Faith in one's total identity with Buddha is a powerful medicine. Huayan texts give us practices to help realize it. For example, they are clear that this realization is dependent on an ethical life. It is impossible to embody Buddhahood while engaging in harm, since Buddhahood is by definition a state of nonharming. Huayan texts also offer many ways to visualize, imagine, and analyze: the four dharmadhatu, true nature and Dharma nature, six characteristics, ten coins, Indra's net, and so forth. They also invite us to meditate and directly see what these teachings point toward.

Huayan texts often refer to cessation and contemplation, also known as *samatha* and *vipassana*—that is, calm abiding and insight, respectively.[144] These terms run throughout Buddhist literature and are interpreted in many ways. Huayan teachings say these are best employed together. Contemplation practices, like the four foundations of mindfulness and Tibetan analytical meditations, involve discernment. Cessation is meditation with no object to focus on and nothing to attain.[145] It is a radical commitment to not objectifying ourselves or our environment, and is a central method of meditation in the Soto Zen and Tibetan Mahamudra traditions. Contemplation and cessation complement each other. It is good to engage the mind to gain insight into what is right here, and it is also good to put down all effort and simply let awareness be what it is, the true source.

Insight can be developed in many ways: through meditation, text study, dialogue, or walks absorbed in Dharma reverie. Likewise, cessation, abiding in the completeness of the moment, can be found anywhere. I came to practice after reading a book by Thich Nhat Hanh called *Peace Is Every Step.* He writes about washing dishes with no object. Thus I have spent a lot of time diving into complex texts with study groups at the Minnesota Zen Meditation Center, and afterward feeling warm soapy water and the smooth edges of cups coming clean. We can practice anywhere, and there are myriad practices. The essayist bell hooks was once asked how she integrates her Buddhist meditation with her feminist practice. She said, "When do I need to reside in that location of stillness and contemplation, and when do I need to get up off my ass and do whatever is needed to be done in terms of physical work, or engagement with others, or confrontation with others? I'm not interested in ranking one type of action over the other."[146]

My life has been transformed by daily meditation, intensive meditation retreats, and the integration of the way of being I find there into my life. This is a common approach to the Buddhist path. I cannot recommend it enough. Many folks, though, arrive through other means. We have a story from the time of the Buddha of a woman who could not give herself to formal practice due to family obligations and the unequal demands placed on her as a woman. She gave herself to the practice in the midst of her domestic life: "One day as she was cooking curry in the kitchen, the meal caught fire and, with a great crackling, burst into flames. In that moment, she had a deep insight into the teaching of impermanence, and she attained the third stage of awakening. From then on, she gave up wearing jewels or ornaments, as if she were already a nun."[147]

James Baldwin said, "we are capable of bearing a great burden, once we discover that the burden is reality, and arrive where reality is."[148] Sometimes, too, what we thought was a burden is no burden at all. To practice and return to where you are is to embody Buddha, naturally pure awareness. Seeing the connection here and now is central to bell hooks's vision of dismantling exploitation. This too is the Huayan way. She once said, "I believe whole-heartedly that the only way out of domination is love, and the only way into really being able to connect with others, and to know how to be, is to be participating in every aspect of your life as a sacrament of love."[149] The *Purifying Practice Sutra* invites us to meet each activity with the wish that everyone be free. We are invited to come home to what is here and to the aspiration for liberation, to the source. This is the way of the bodhisattva, meeting everything with compassion by seeing through alienation; of Sudhana, arriving at the wonder of each moment; and of the Buddha, walking slowly, eating food he begged for, knowing the breath in the body, and sitting in the forest talking with folks about their ability to be free.

24

Seeing Through It All

破息妄想必不得

Without ending delusion it is surely not attained.

"I was standing in the rain and I could feel every single droplet meet my skin." "I was walking through my neighborhood and suddenly I was everyone I saw." "I looked up at a waning moon and time disappeared." "I was sitting listening to the wind, and then there was no me to listen to the wind. There was just the wind." "The grief became a realization that we could never be apart." "The entire universe was that little frog in the grass looking up." "I can't describe it, nothing changed, and everything was completely different." I have heard many words like these. In his classic *Varieties of Religious Experience*, William James says that one of the pervasive features of powerful spiritual experiences is that they are ineffable. It is difficult to describe something whose fundamental characteristic is that it is beyond the categories that language creates. Huayan teachings show this truth by using language. They provide a dizzying array of ways to think about, view, and realize our indescribably complete interdependence.

The previous line of our text was about practice, and this one is about realization. If you practice and return to the true source—this very moment of sight, sound, smell, taste, touch, and mind—you can end delusion and attain the Ocean Seal Samadhi. You can be in the true source, where you already are. As long as we remain caught by our limited views, that we are separate entities moving through an environment, we will bear and create the pains of samsara. This text begins with and constantly reiterates that this moment is of Dharma nature: harmonious, round, complete, seamless, without characteristic, peaceful. It also of true nature: subtle, profound, arising dependent on conditions, where one is all and many are one. Here, though, the text is explicit in saying that we will not truly know it unless we end delusion. Practice leads somewhere. It leads to experience, which is liberation from suffering for all. Attainment here means actualizing liberation from suffering with your body and mind. We can realize liberation, and we can make it real.

In Buddhist teachings, there are three root poisons: desire, aversion, and delusion. All manner of secondary afflictions relate back to them. For example, anger, laziness, and deceitfulness are aspects of aversion. Early Buddhist texts tend to emphasize ending the afflictive emotions—desire and aversion—while Mahayana texts emphasize ending delusion as most fundamental. I have written quite a bit about how Yogacara texts show a powerful way to integrate these two polarities.[150] In short, being mindful of and showing care for afflictive emotions as they arise is powerful medicine. However, our text follows a common Mahayana reasoning: if we end delusion, the other afflictions fall away.

When we are deluded, we don't see the true nature of things, that because they arise dependently each thing contains all. We don't see the Dharma nature, nameless, without characteristic, harmonious, and peaceful. In his commentary on this line, Pobyung says that delusion here refers to the view that there is a self and other things. This is called *dvayagraha* in Yogacara texts and is understood to be the fundamental delusion we must overcome.[151] In another comment, Uisang refers to the *Lion's Roar of Queen Srimala* (the *Srimaladevi Sutra*). This sutra says delusion is the inability to see that we each have *tathagata garbha*, which is the capacity for awakening, and an already awakened nature. The term literally means "womb of the tathagatas," another name for Buddha nature, which is merely obscured by passing afflictions that are not our true nature.

Thus Hakuin wrote that we are like, "someone in the midst of water, crying out in thirst."[152] In the *Gandavyuha Sutra*, we meet a crowd of hungry ghosts standing on the bank of the wide-flowing Ganges, desperately looking to find water, but seeing only ashes in a dry riverbed.[153] The promise of this tradition is that we can feel the cool of the water on our skin, on our tongues, in our throats, taste it, know it sustaining us from down in our bellies, delight in its healing power, know that we are mostly water, know that the water that is us fills the sky, the rivers, and the oceans, is the bodies of others, ourselves. Water is life. It is not bound. It flows.

The eightfold path and the paramitas lead to the end of delusion. We can follow the basic teaching that holds them all: do no harm, cultivate the good, and train the mind. We can integrate meditation and ethical conduct. We can learn to embody the truth that is right here. Huayan texts spin out complex visualizations and ways to see the world. They offer practices for ending delusion. They are complex and varied specifically to remind us that the path is long and the methods for ending delusion are as varied as each individual moment.

Attaining realization matters. Ending delusion matters. I used to believe that alcohol and drugs were the only things I could rely on. The suffering I caused living from that belief was immense. Letting go of that delusion was a tiny drop in an ocean of liberation. What more is possible? What further delusions may we shed? May we all practice to end the delusions that bind us together in the grinding wheel of samsara. May we realize that we are the heirs of our actions and the ancestors of the future. Women are giving birth at this very moment to children whose lives depend on what we do.

25

Unconditional Love

無緣善巧捉如意

Unconditional skillful means bring wish fulfillment.

Sujata saw a man beneath a tree, emaciated, exhausted, near death. He had set forth on a quest to end suffering, and had wracked his body with austerities in the belief that this would be the path to freedom. She brought him milk-rice pudding. Though he had committed to going beyond earthly sustenance and avoiding young women, he accepted the gift.[154] That giving, the gift, and the willingness to accept it was the gate that the man walked through to find the Middle Way, to realize he was awake, Buddha. Without this simple moment of intimacy, there would be no Buddhism. The people in this story manifested spontaneous, natural wisdom and kindness.

In his commentary on this line, Pobyung says it refers to a capacity to promote well-being that is not conditioned. Unconditional skillful means are not skills that we acquire, like the ability to speak a language, write code, or make furniture. They are the natural, harmonious response to the moment when we are not bound by fixed views. If we focus more on seeing clearly and less on plans and strategies, something beautiful can happen. This line invites faith that in this moment something can naturally arise that is good for everyone and everything. It can arise in the form of how we speak, think, and move our bodies. It can be what we do.

On the one hand, this is a way of saying that skillful means are of Dharma nature, they arise dependent on the wisdom of Buddha, which is the absence of separation. Practically speaking, this can help us to not be overwhelmed, feeling we need to acquire all the proper skills for saving beings. To realize unconditional skillful means is to trust the moment or, as Uchiyama Roshi says, to "open the hand of thought." All of the odd behavior that we find in the records of Zen—the startling shouts, expletives, jokes, songs, Gutei's one-finger Zen, and Satsujo sitting on the *Lotus Sutra*—they all celebrate these unconditional skillful means.

This is Huayan. It's nondual, so celebrating unconditional skillful means doesn't mean we shouldn't also develop conditioned skillful means. Yes, let us learn to knit, cook, prescribe medicines, understand Dharma, sing, listen, be still, install solar panels, perform rituals. Each of the teachers that Sudhana meets has a particular path and way of freeing beings that they have developed. Sudhana meets each with wonder and reverence. We really don't know, though, if he is acquiring or accumulating anything. He just keeps meeting the moment with a loving heart.

In the Pali Canon the Buddha teaches, "There is, monks, an unborn, unbecome, unmade, unconditioned. If there were no unborn, unbecome, unmade, unconditioned, no escape would be discerned from what is born, become, made, conditioned."[155] In Huayan, escape from the conditioned is deemphasized. The relationship between the conditioned and unconditioned is heightened. The opportunity to manifest a spontaneous beneficial response to the moment is celebrated.

Cesar Chavez once said, "There is no such thing as defeat in nonviolence."[156] You can't lose, and you can't beat anyone. Nonviolence is an ethic rooted in awareness that seeing people and things as others drives our whole cycle of suffering. Dr. King once said, "at the center of nonviolence stands the principle of love."[157] Because there is an unconditioned, there are no objects. We can act from unconditional love, the awareness that there is nothing to control. We can't own this capacity, and I don't think anyone manifests it perfectly. Many who have done it beautifully have also done great harm. Nevertheless, there have been upwellings of powerful, effective skillful means throughout history, based on an utterly improbable willingness to meet violence with love. Gandhi formulated his theory and practice on the idea of *satya*, truth. When we see the truth, what is there is nonviolence. This realization can happen spontaneously. In World War I, on Christmas Day, 1914, thousands of soldiers who had been brutally killing each other rose from their trenches, sang, and exchanged gifts on the very ground where they would soon again wage war.

In his "Letter from Birmingham Jail," Dr. King describes something that has been embodied throughout the history of nonviolent direct action: it takes practice. He says that before you enter the field, you must engage in what he called "self-purification." I pray we may realize the natural unconditioned capacity for nonviolence, for skillful means to free all beings. I pray we may commit to the practices that create them.

The *Avatamsaka Sutra* constantly extolls the virtues of manifesting compassion regardless of conditions. Its opening chapter keeps returning to the bodhisattva's four methods of guidance: "giving, kind speech, beneficial action, and cooperation."[158] These are skillful means that bring people the treasure they truly want: well-being. In differing traditions these show up with slight variations. In the Pali Canon, the first three are the same, and the fourth is "consistency in the face of events."[159]

For Dogen, the fourth is "identity action." Dogen says the fourth method is action that emerges from seeing that each thing is not different from each other thing.[160] This is the fourth dharmadhatu I addressed in chapter 17. If we look at the three different terms for the fourth method of guidance, we can see a clear relationship between cooperation, consistency in the face of events, and identity action. By seeing through alienation, a bodhisattva engages in cooperation with a joy and compassion that is not dependent on conditions. Giving, kind speech, beneficial action, and cooperation are the shapes in which the unconditional wisdom and compassion of the bodhisattva spontaneously show up.

In my community, the days after George Floyd was murdered were full of anguish, confusion, and rage. As the faces of my beloved colleagues of the Multifaith Anti-Racism, Change & Healing (MARCH) Minnesota clergy group popped onto the screen for our online meeting, the exhaustion and despair were already palpable. Friends who had been working to end racism and police brutality for decades were faced with a fresh horror. As a person of European descent, I had no idea what to say to my African American friends. How could we even begin the meeting? What was the work to be done? One of my colleagues decided. We must watch a video of Prince singing "Starfish and Coffee" with the Muppets. Three minutes, a lot of chair dancing, Zoom-muted singing, smiles, and tears later, we knew we loved each other, we knew we were there to do the work of love, and we got to work on planning our next steps.

26

How to Act in Eden

歸家隨分得資糧

Returning home, effortlessly gaining treasures,

We are invited to come home, to find a place of refuge, comfort, and rest. In his commentary on this line, Uisang writes, "What does 'home' mean? It means a shady covering and a place where one abides. . . . Because the skillful [expedient means] of great compassion cover living beings in a shady manner it is called a 'house.'"[161] Our practice can bring us to a place of ease and repose. It can itself be ease and repose. Shitou's "Song of the Grass Roof Hermitage" says, "Just sitting with head covered, all things are at rest."[162] In any moment you can bring your attention to whatever emotion is present without needing to fix, judge, or control. This is a natural manifestation of compassion. We can learn to rest in the shade of this compassion. We can extend it to the whole field of awareness. Just now I pause for buzzing insects, voices from the street, feet on the cool floor, the icons on my altar, the fading scent of sage. In previous lines, Uisang exhorted us to practice, to end delusion. Here we are invited into effortlessness. Many musicians, athletes, hikers, lovers, and parents know this effortlessness. We give ourselves to our practices, and sometimes it is hard, but sometimes the music just emerges, the kindness is unforced, mountains and rivers do not block your way, but instead they are your way.

The *Dhammapada* says, "I have seen you, housebuilder; you shall not build this house again. Its beams are broken; its dome is shattered: self-will is extinguished; nirvana is attained."[163] In many Buddhist traditions, ordination is known as home-leaving. Early Buddhists left home to travel Northern India on foot with no fixed abode. Nowadays home-leaving often means moving to a monastery, or may be a metaphorical leaving behind of old ways. In Buddhist practice we leave the rickety home of fixed ideas to come home to what is right here. In the ten ox-herding pictures representing the path of Zen, the final stage of practice is to return home, to the marketplace, with bliss-bestowing hands. There are many ways to find refuge. Buddhist traditions all share the idea that we can find true refuge in Buddha, Dharma, and Sangha, and leave behind the many ways we look for refuge that don't really help us all to be safe. There is so much we can leave behind—so many habits, possessions, desires, irritations, fears. There is so much to come home to, for this very moment is always complete. The Chan nun Daoqian wrote:

You've been earnestly studying the Way year after year
And now no longer cling to either existence nor
non-existence.
But having come home you should not just sit around,
But instead go out and till the fields of merit for
others.[164]

Uisang, Pobyung, and Kyunyo all write comments on this line. They say the terms *treasure* and *wealth* that we see throughout the text refer to practice conducive to enlightenment. Our poem keeps telling us we are receiving jewels, riches, treasures. The true treasure is the ability to practice for liberation. In his first teaching on the four noble truths, the Buddha shows that we can always act in a way that leads to nirvana. Uisang refers to wealth as "assisting bodhi," assisting awakening. Although Dharma nature is all-pervading, we can help. We can take care of Buddha. Within nonduality we can take care of what's here in this moment without viewing anything as an object to control or an outcome to gain. Thich Nhat Hanh invited us to care for each thing as if we were bathing a baby Buddha. What about an elderly Buddha, or one who has passed away? With reverence and care, things don't need to seem like chores. I have seen profound ease in folks cooking food for their children, in ringing huge temple bells long before dawn, in painting a banner for a march supporting bold action to stem climate change. I saw such reverence, such natural energy, as thousands of us walked singing down a highway to protect the precious waters of the Mississippi and the indigenous Anishinaabe people.

Pobyung equates "assisting bodhi" with the thirty-seven aids to enlightenment: the four foundations of mindfulness, the fourfold right effort, the four bases of power, the five faculties, the five powers, the seven factors of enlightenment, and the noble eightfold path. Our text is nearing its climax, inviting us into a shady home built of vast compassion, a home where with no effort we naturally offer practice that helps us all be free. With this invitation, Uisang invokes a comprehensive list of Buddhist practices that we can cultivate. Right now we can be mindful of the breath, of the posture, of desire, energy, ill will, discernment, and tranquility. We can see whatever is here. Right now, we can make an effort so that wellness arises and suffering fades. We can practice the path. When this effort arises with no effort, we have arrived at home.

27

Letting It Be Magic

以陀羅尼無盡寶

Through dharani, an inexhaustible treasure

Two cubs ran across the trail ahead. Scanning from left to right I saw her, a mother grizzly, her head turned to stare straight at our little crew. We were on retreat, en route from camp to Stoney Indian Pass, high above the Mokowanis River valley on Blackfeet land occupied by the United States. She was focused. The cubs rallied around her, but she was dead still, massive, gazing our way. We backed up a bit, and she and the cubs crossed back over the trail and downslope, past a patch of huckleberries and into thicker woods. We moved forward toward the pass, and to get out of their space. As we walked, one of our members began to chant the Disaster Protection Dharani. Singing or speaking keeps bears and people safe when you move through grizzly country. It helps us all to know where we are, to avoid startling one another. A couple hundred yards down the trail we paused and offered the merit of the chanting, the power of the ancient spell of protection, to the safety and well-being of the mother and cubs we met along the path.

Early in his commentary, Uisang says that by *dharani* he means Buddhist teachings—that is, Dharma. It is the Dharma that brings inexhaustible treasure, skillful means, to help folks be free. Recall, though, that dharanis are generally short texts, sometimes almost meaningless ones, which carry the power of the Dharma. Rather than teaching something discursively, they create the opportunity to voice the power of the Dharma more directly. Personally, I've never felt a connection to Christian theology, but I have tasted the joy, mercy, and surrender of the tradition while dancing and singing in church and at rallies for justice. Dharanis and chanting can similarly bring the presence, compassion, healing, and connection of the Dharma to where we are right now. Uisang's "Song of Dharma Nature" is written to be chanted, to be taken into the voice and body. You may sing its wonders into being.

In Korea, for hundreds of years, images of this text and the text itself have been used as a means to evoke inexhaustible treasures. Using this text and others like it to evoke goodness, safety, and completeness is a powerful practice. The fearlessness and compassion of bodhisattvas is not dependent on getting the right conditions; it is meeting the conditions of right now with the inexhaustible treasure of skillful means. Our text and this Ocean Seal Chart are meant to help us feel this fearlessness and compassion. I have kept a copy of this text on the wall above my desk for a couple years. It has helped me. You may take up the practice of using this text as a spell of protection, a way to attract inexhaustible treasures through dharani.

This book has been an investigation into the meanings of this text, but the text itself can also be known, not in relation to external meaning, but as an immediate experience. What is it like to chant it now? The liberation it promises, the inexhaustible treasure, isn't somewhere else or in some meaning outside of now.

In the *Avatamsaka*, Sudhana finds the bodhisattva Avalokiteshvara sitting high in a mountain glen, teaching love and compassion. Avalokiteshvara teaches that people can gain protection from countless calamities: prisons, bandits, wild animals, rushing rivers, demons, from violence, and from doing violent things. He says we can gain this protection merely by remembering his name.[165] We may invoke Avalokiteshvara and Kannon, the male and female names for the one who hears the cries of the world. Perhaps kneel, like one person recently described to me, before an altar with Kannon and feel the healing balm of telling her your troubles. Myriad people have found the strength to keep going through faith by invoking the names of great beings. We need countless means to meet the perils of alienation and paralyzing or reactive fear. The ability to act for the well-being of all is a gift, but like the gift of a flower in spring, we must prepare the ground.

28

The Golden Lion

莊嚴法界實寶殿

Adorns the Dharma realm, a true jeweled palace.

Our practice is to adorn something unutterably precious and beautiful, to strew flowers in a field of flowers, to pour compassion into an ocean of compassion. This kind of teaching seemed utterly foreign to my experience when I began practice. I was trying to fix my broken self in an awful world. I was consumed by bouts of rage and despair. I could be terribly unkind. My mind streamed with hateful thoughts about myself. To say that my moments of experience were good, that the world was good, that I had the capacity for goodness, seemed like a cruel joke. Yet somehow these teachings made a crack in my fixed views, in the thick haze of afflictive emotion. I would listen to people with full attention and realize that I was offering something precious. I would lengthen my spine, breathe into the belly, and notice that I was not broken. I could look into the tired face of a fellow recovering addict, or imagine the raging cornered wolf in my heart as I received treatment for posttraumatic stress, or see the yellow sunlight streaming through the trees at dusk, and there I could see some peace and goodness. We have beautiful gardens at our Zen center. I realized I had become part of the community when I was asked to help install a bicycle rack. The bike rack is still there, with my bike on it—adornments in the Dharma realm.

At various points in the *Avatamsaka Sutra* people bring vast troves of jewels out of the earth with a mere gesture or wish. Fazang describes adorning the realm as acting according to truth and virtue, embodying the paramitas, and awakening. The teachers in the *Gandavyuha* show that there are many ways to adorn the realm. I am so grateful for all the gorgeous gardens; the songs that flow through my neighborhood in summer; for the luminaria lighting the night in the deep dark of the northern winter; for all the paintings, songs, dances, quilts; for the leaves turning to flame in the vast woods in autumn in Minnesota; for the two sunflowers from our garden sitting on the altar next to Katagiri Roshi's memorial tablet, who faced me as I offered bows this morning. I offered bows for wisdom and compassion, and to pledge to repair any harms that brought me here. How will you adorn the realm?

Robin Wall Kimmerer wrote, "Paying attention is a form of reciprocity with the living world, receiving the gifts with open eyes and open heart."[166] In the *Avatamsaka*, Sudhana travels to learn from the girl Maitrayani in a hall filled with townspeople. He asks her how to do the practice of a bodhisattva. She says, "Look around."

He looks at the pillars, the people, the banners, and sees Buddha. Then she says she has perfected the practice of "facing in all directions."[167] I invite you into her practice, as she invites Sudhana. Right now, to hear all sounds, to see all sights, to smell all scents, to taste all tastes, to feel the whole body, to know all that is mind, all the emotions. Developing open awareness through meditation is a gateway to seeing the Buddha in each thing. To see beauty and preciousness is to create beauty and preciousness.

Fazang gave one of the most famous teachings of Huayan to Empress Wu. He pointed to a golden lion, a guardian statue outside the hall. He said that each thing is made of gold, is inseparable from the gold, and the gold can only manifest as particular things.[168] This teaching equates gold with *li*, the universal, and the lion and its parts with *shi*, the particular. The comparison is similar to others: water and waves, sky and clouds, mirror and images.

The text of the teaching of the golden lion uses these basic elements to illustrate ten points: (1) dependent arising, (2) the distinction between form and emptiness, (3) the Yogacara teaching of the three natures,[169] (4) the nonexistence of forms, (5) the unborn, (6) Fazang's fivefold classification of Buddhist schools, (7) Zhiyan's teaching on ten mysterious gates to realization,[170] (8) embracing the six senses, (9) attainment of awakening, and (10) entering nirvana.

Again, we see the Huayan celebration of the number ten. Zhiyan's ten mysterious gates is in itself an exhaustive investigation into the relationship between li and shi. Zhiyan wrote that the use of complex lists of ten is to show that the teaching is inexhaustible. Mahayana teachings on emptiness are hard to grasp, if not impossible, because their purpose is to bring you to an awareness where there is nothing to grasp and thus no grasping. Huayan teachings are long and expansive in order to invite you into practice with no limit. None of this is about figuring it all out.

The pith, though, of the golden lion teaching is that each thing is of immeasurable value. We can see the universe in each thing, and each thing as part of an unbroken whole. When we see a world that is made of objects to be used, we stray from practicing the way, and we don't adorn the Dharma realm. Rather than facing in all directions, we see only what our habits and our self-centering show us. We carelessly tear down the banners of Maitrayani's hall, we bump roughly through the people listening at her feet. The earth is not an object to be used, and we are not powerless in the face of the tendency to see it as one. People are not resources to be extracted, and we can divest from exploitation. To practice seeing this and to act from this awareness is to plant native seeds on native soil in a garden of native flowers.

29

All Things at Rest

窮坐實際中道床

Just sitting in the bed of the Middle Way,
the ultimate reality,

The first teaching of the Buddha, so the story goes, was the Middle Way. In the *Discourse on Setting the Wheel of Dharma in Motion* he offers two definitions of the Middle Way: first, avoiding the extremes of self-mortification and pursuing sensual pleasure, and second, practicing the eightfold path: right view, intention, speech, action, livelihood, effort, mindfulness, and concentration.[171] Later Mahayana texts say that the Middle Way is seeing that things appear dependent on relative views, but are also empty of all the characteristics that they appear to have. This verse invites us to realize the embodiment of the eightfold path, the way between extremes, as a place of stillness, ease, and clear seeing. Just sitting in ultimate reality does not sound like a lot of work or a major accomplishment. Can you actually be somewhere other than reality?

In his commentary on this line, Uisang focuses on the Mahayana view of the Middle Way. If things are empty of separate existence, they don't come into being and they don't abide. He says not abiding is the middle path.[172] It is possible to see through the idea that the me that was here a few minutes ago is the me that's here now. The me that is here now won't be here in the next minute. There is a total freshness in this moment where practice—that is, unconditional skillful means—can arise. My teacher is constantly telling stories of his teacher, Shunryu Suzuki Roshi, responding to situations in surprising, disarming, and liberating ways. My friend and Dharma teacher Jon Aaron was facing a major surgery, and as he told me about it, although there was some fear, I mostly heard curiosity, wonder, and gratitude. There was little sense that there was a healthier version of himself that was supposed to be continuing from the past, or a present self that needed to last in the face of aging. The sense that this moment was *the* moment was so strong that it filled both of us as it flowed from his practice between and around us.

Some translators render the last character of this line, 床, as *couch* or *throne* rather than *bed*. The character is ambiguous. Just sitting can occur wherever you are. This line may describe a state of rest in the vastness of reality, a great Buddhist adept sitting on a Dharma throne, or you, the reader, sitting on a simple couch. These are not ultimately separate.

Just sitting is the most central practice that Katagiri Roshi and Suzuki Roshi transmitted to the people who share my Dharma lineage. Dogen Zenji, our Soto Zen founder, extols the practice of just sitting, sometimes called *shikantaza*, in majestically transcendent terms. To sit with the body upright, the hands in a mudra, with the eyes open and gazing slightly down is complete practice. There are myriad techniques and approaches to sitting meditation, but here one is at rest. Earlier Chan teachers called it silent illumination. Shitou says of this practice, "Let go of hundreds of years and relax completely." When I practice with Mingyur Rinpoche, we receive this Mahamudra teaching: "not meditating and not distracted, awareness relaxes into itself."

In this line of our text, though, there is no mention of mind. Here is a body in a place of repose, ultimate reality. This text is trying to give us enough faith to trust in the completeness of the simplest of meditation practices, just sitting with no object we are trying to focus on, no goal we are trying to achieve. We may find ourselves just sitting in the bed of the Middle Way—that is, ultimate reality. We may need to make a little effort to find our way to a cushion to sit down. We may find that wherever we are sitting is a fresh moment where we can manifest the Middle Way, a path of liberation from suffering. With practice, we may find that any moment can be a place where all things are at rest, like a wise grandparent calmly, firmly, and kindly responding to the tumult of a home full of work, arguments, tantrums, and play.

30

Buddha Is Still Here

舊來不動名爲佛

This original stillness is named Buddha.

As you finish chanting Uisang's "Song of Dharma Nature," sitting in the posture of meditation, your voice intones this line: "This original stillness is Buddha." The stillness that pervades this moment is Buddha, and this has always been true. The practice of meditation, chanting, or ritual often produces a sense of stillness, but even when it does not, the stillness, primordial, is here. Recall the second line of our song, "All dharmas are unmoving, fundamentally peaceful." Habits of perception, of mind, make it appear as though things move, things come and go, but they are not showing us the whole truth. They hide the utter stillness, the nirvana, that is here. Our text is an invitation to have enough faith to practice the Buddha way so that we may realize this.

In the Ocean Seal Chart, the text ends in the middle, exactly where it started. The last character of the text is 佛,

Buddha, while the first is 法, Dharma. We travel through thirty lines of Uisang's song and arrive at the beginning. In his commentary on this line, Pobyung says it is like a person who falls asleep, travels to thirty post offices, and wakes up knowing that he never left his bed. In our lives we travel, sufferings and joys come and go, and we can also realize that we have always been right here. We may think that the dream is false and the waking is real, but both of them matter, for they are our lives. The *Avatamsaka* offers the simile of someone who falls asleep and sees staggeringly inspiring visions of liberation while those awake around him do not. In the same way, the sutra says bodhisattvas see the power of Buddha that is right here while others do not.[173]

The *Avatamsaka* says, "There is not a single sentient being who is not fully endowed with the knowledge of Buddha." It says, "The sphere of mind is the sphere of Buddha. Just as the sphere of mind is measureless and boundless, without bondage or liberation, so too is the sphere of Buddhas measureless and boundless without bondage or liberation." It says, "The emptiness of inherent nature is Buddha."[174] The great Yogacarin Dignaga wrote, "It is the naturally pure cognition of ordinary beings that is expressed by the term 'buddha.'"[175] *Cognition* here refers to seeing, hearing, tasting, thinking, feeling, smelling, and feeling like a self that is separate from all these things. It refers to the whole of this moment of perception. We can see through all the divisions and see a seamless stillness.

In his comments on this line, Uisang embraces a fundamental paradox of Mahayana Buddhism: you are already in nirvana, and you can practice to be free from samsara. Suffering is often so vivid. We despair, we are irritated, we hanker, we rage, we judge. Perhaps we feel good but see others in the throes of addiction, oppression, anxiety. We may feel sorrow for the trees, the soil, the kittens, the oceans, the fish, and the whales. Our text has invited us to see that we have skillful means to make some beneficial offering. Our lives matter, suffering matters, and our practice matters. Each of us has the opportunity, a precious jewel, to find our way.

Yesterday in a class I was teaching, students were reflecting on the experience of reading the *Avatamsaka*. One remarked that its relentless repetition of the word *joy*, and of joyful images and qualities, had infused their experience during their week of study. We can fill our moments with this good medicine. Maya Angelou wrote, "You are the sum total of everything you've ever seen, heard, eaten, smelled, been told, forgot—it's all there. Everything influences each of us, and because of that I try to make sure that my experiences are positive."[176]

Uisang's text does not focus on suffering and healing. It's OK—lots of Buddhist texts do that! This one invites us to see that within one is all, that nirvana is here, that our aspiration for awakening is precious, that our capacity to be compassionate is a gift that always arrives if we care to open it. Just seeing what is here is compassion. You don't need to make some special kind of mind. To be compassionate is to be with suffering. The text invites us to have the courage to be still and really see, and then to return home, to take a step, say a beneficial word, give some money, do the laundry, build community, care for the earth and each other.

Just sitting under a tree, Buddha realized a stillness that was unconditioned, a peace that was not dependent on anything. This peace came from seeing how things depend on one another. He claimed that this peace never left him, and that when he died, he would be neither gone nor here.[177] The stillness he saw came from seeing that our dualistic ways of looking at things is one-sided. It never shows the whole truth. In the primordial stillness that the Buddha found, he spent years traveling the country. He lived on food he begged for, he meditated, and he offered help to those who asked for it. We have stories of him going on retreat and knowing his breathing, of setting out to meet a mass murderer, of counseling kings to give away their wealth and to refrain from war. We have stories of him supporting the shattered, the traumatized, and the grieving, the poor, the rich, the old, the young, the hale, and the dying. He counseled monks to help the hungry find food, to create time in silence to focus on meditation. He supported many whose practice had brought them profound peace and were looking to take one more step toward seeing the stillness that is here.

In the final pages of the *Avatamsaka* we find this verse:

As long as earth exists,
As long as all beings exist,
As long as acts and afflictions exist,
So long will my vow remain.[178]

The bodhisattva vow is undying. It's not somewhere else. It belongs to no one. May we listen for its song, its invitation. May it live in our voices, in our bodies, and in our hearts. The stillness that is Buddha is a life of compassionate action.

Acknowledgments

I am grateful for the precious opportunity to give myself to this study and writing, for your kind attention, for your support. I am grateful for the great ancestors who opened the Buddha Way, too many to name: Shakyamuni Buddha, Mahapajapati, Vasubandhu, Dogen, Miaozong; to Samantabhadra on his white elephant striding along in unimaginable possibility; to Buddha Vairocana everywhere; to Kannon, essence of compassion.

My teacher Tim Burkett first brought me to study Huayan; Thich Nhat Hanh's embodiment of engaged Buddhism inspired by Huayan called me deeper; and Jin Y. Park's pointing me to Uisang's Ocean Seal Chart opened the way for this book. I offer bows to you all.

This book is entirely dependent on the efforts of academics and scholar-practitioners who offer the precious work of translation and deep study. Thomas Cleary in particular has transformed my life, and Richard McBride's work with the Ocean Seal Chart has been an invaluable resource. To Francis H. Cook, Bhikshu Dharmamitra, Garma C.C. Chang, Robert Gimello, Peter Gregory, Imre Hamar, Ruben Habito, Hee Sung Keel, Dae Heng Sunim,

Charlie Pokorny, Mu Soeng, Judith Simmer-Brown, and Dale S. Wright, I offer bows. Their insights are profound, and any errors in this book are my own.

To my longtime partner in translation, Weijen Teng. I offer deep thanks. What fortune to have found you on my path and share in your keen insight! I offer a bow.

To the early readers of this book for their generous support, Ruben Habito, Mushim Patricia Ikeda, Taigen Dan Leighton, Rhonda Magee, Sue Moon, and Judith Simmer-Brown. I offer a bow.

To Sehee Kim and Jihyun Kim of the Jungto Society, Chang-Seong Hong, Sinwoo, and Mushim Patricia Ikeda, who offered personal insights on Korean Buddhism, I offer a bow of gratitude for your generosity.

To all the Japanese folks who brought Soto Zen to North American shores, and to all the folks from Asia who crossed oceans and shared the Dharma here in any way. I offer a bow.

To Dainin and Tomoe Katagiri, who planted the seeds of Dharma here in my neighborhood that flourish and nurture so many. Deep bows.

To the Indigenous people of North America for their clear message that I, of European descent, am on stolen land. To the Dakota and Anishinaabe, who have cared for the land where I live for so long, for their calls to repair the harm that settlers and their descendants have done. I offer a bow and a pledge of action.

To my beloved colleagues at Wisdom Publications,

Laura Cunningham, Ben Gleason, and Daniel Aitken, for your care and support of my writing.

Dear friends on the path are the path. To all my Minnesota Zen Meditation Center friends, but in particular to Tim Burkett, Ted O'Toole, Susan Nelson, Rosemary Taylor, Bussho Lahn, and Bonnie Versbonceour, I offer a bow. To all of our community, you bring the Dharma alive for me.

For your heartfelt support as I wrote this book: Pamela Ayo Yetunde, Koshin Paley Ellison, Gyokei Yokoyama, and Robert Chodo Campbell, great gratitude.

To all the people who support me in traveling to teach, who bring me to your practice centers. For me, it's always about relationship, and I am grateful to be included. I bow to you.

To folks at Minnesota Multifaith Network, Multifaith Anti-Racist Change and Healing, Minnesota Interfaith Power and Light, Soto Zen Buddhist Association, GenX Dharma Teachers, to all the water protectors, the Indigenous folks who are building the movement, to everyone at George Floyd Square, everyone working for real public safety that is not state violence, it is with you that I realize the way. I offer a bow.

To all the folks in addiction recovery, the therapists who have been my friends, my colleagues, and my life raft when I was drowning. Here is my undying gratitude and a bow.

To my parents, sibling, and children: Karin, Peter, Chris, Rock, Del, Finn, Max, and Daisy. I love you more than I can ever say or even do, but I'll keep trying. To my beloved Colleen. There is no me without you, and this will always be true.

Notes

1 Kimmerer, *Braiding Sweetgrass*, 330.
2 Ñāṇamoli, *Middle Length Discourses*, 307–12.
3 Hamar, *Reflecting Mirrors*, 118.
4 Dharmamitra, *Flower Adornment Sutra*, 323.
5 Dharmamitra, *Flower Adornment Sutra*, 326.
6 *Soto School Scriptures for Daily Services and Practice* (Tokyo: Sotoshu Shumucho and the Soto Zen Text Project, 2001), 73.
7 Thich Nhat Hạnh, *Present Moment Wonderful Moment*, rev. ed. (Berkeley, CA: Parallax Press, 2022), 7.
8 Keel, *Chinul*, 49.
9 Cleary, *Entry Into the Inconceivable*.
10 Dharmamitra, *Flower Adornment Sutra*, 1786.
11 Cleary, *Flower Ornament Scripture*, 1222–23.
12 Hamar, *Reflecting Mirrors*, 302.
13 Korean Buddhist Research Institute, *The History and Culture of Buddhism in Korea* (Seoul, South Korea: Dongguk University Press, 1993), 91.
14 Mu Soeng, *Thousand Peaks*, 49–50.
15 This video provides audio of Korean chanting of the text of the Beopseongge while the path of text through the Ocean Seal Chart is illustrated with a moving red line: https://www.youtube.com/watch?v=n42qv8Whz-M.
16 McBride, *Collected Works of Korean Buddhism*, 21.
17 McBride, *Collected Works of Korean Buddhism*, 54.
18 McBride, *Collected Works of Korean Buddhism*, 71.
19 McBride, *Collected Works of Korean Buddhism*, 111.
20 Hamar, *Reflecting Mirrors*, 300.
21 https://www.youtube.com/watch?v=vPJ3nIfM59w.
22 McBride, "Dharani and Mantra in Contemporary Korean Buddhism," 385, 390, 394, 398.

23 Grant, *Daughters of Emptiness*, 129.
24 Bodhi, *In the Buddha's Words*, 366.
25 Cleary, *Flower Ornament Scripture*, 380.
26 Liu Ming-Wood, "The 'P'an-chiao' System of the Hua-yen School in Chinese Buddhism," 40.
27 McBride, *Collected Works of Korean Buddhism*, 192.
28 Ñāṇamoli, *Middle Length Discourses*, 711.
29 Powers, *Wisdom of Buddha*, 103.
30 Cleary, *Flower Ornament Scripture*, 637.
31 Gimello, *Chih-Yeh and the Foundations of Hua-Yen Buddhism*, 474.
32 Garfield, *Fundamental Wisdom of the Middle Way*, 10.
33 Cleary, *Entry Into the Inconceivable*, 55.
34 Leighton, *Cultivating the Empty Field*, 72.
35 Ñāṇamoli, *Middle Length Discourses*, 297.
36 Cleary, *Flower Ornament Scripture*, 300.
37 Hamar, *Reflecting Mirrors*, 250.
38 *The Śūraṅgama Sūtra: A New Translation* (Ukiah, CA: Buddhist Text Translation Society, 2017), 209.
39 Cleary, *Blue Cliff Record*, 428.
40 Ferguson, *Zen's Chinese Heritage*, 271.
41 Cheng Chien Bhikshu, *Manifestation of the Tathagata* (Boston: Wisdom Publications, 1993), 34–40.
42 Gimello, *Chih-Yeh and the Foundations of Hua-Yen Buddhism*, 3.
43 Park, *Buddhism and Postmodernity*, 6.
44 hooks, *All About Love*, 93.
45 Cleary, *Entry Into the Inconceivable*, 79.
46 hooks, *Ain't I a Woman?*, 157.
47 Kimmerer, *Braiding Sweetgrass*, 104.
48 Quoted in Kirsten Karchmer, *Seeing Red: The One Book Every Woman Needs to Read. Period.* (New York: S&S / Simon Element, 2019), 87.
49 Grant, *Zen Echoes*, 111.
50 Cleary, *Entry Into the Inconceivable*, 146.
51 Cleary, *Entry Into the Inconceivable*, 157–58.
52 Caplow and Moon, *Hidden Lamp*, 253.
53 Murcott, *First Buddhist Women*, 18.
54 *Karaniya Metta Sutta*, Sn 1.8, from https://www.accesstoinsight.org/tipitaka/kn/snp/snp.1.08.amar.html.

55 Caplow and Moon, *Hidden Lamp*, 107.
56 Cheng Chien Bhikshu, *Manifestation of the Tathāgata*, 39.
57 hooks, *All About Love*, 153.
58 *Soto School Scriptures for Daily Services and Practice*, 30.
59 From Robert E. Buswell Jr., trans., *The Korean Approach to Zen: The Collected Works of Chinul* (Honolulu: University of Hawaii Press, 1983), 24; quoted in Mu Soeng, *Thousand Peaks*, 89.
60 Cleary, *Flower Ornament Scripture*, 1462.
61 Murcott, *First Buddhist Women*, 85.
62 Quoted in Editors of *Freedomways*, *Paul Robeson: The Great Forerunner* (New York: International Publishers, 1998), 235.
63 Liu Ming-Wood, "The 'P'an-chiao' System of the Hua-yen School in Chinese Buddhism," 28.
64 Chang, *Buddhist Teaching of Totality*, 24.
65 Fannin, Coleman, *30-Day Journey with Dorothy Day* (Minneapolis: Fortress Press, 2019), 16.
66 Cleary, *Flower Ornament Scripture*, 1022.
67 Cleary, *Entry Into the Inconceivable*, 157.
68 Chang, *Buddhist Teaching of Totality*, 24.
69 Cleary, *Entry Into the Inconceivable*, 134.
70 Wright, "The 'Thought of Enlightenment' in Fa-tsang's Hua-yen Buddhism," 99.
71 Tanahashi, *Moon in a Dewdrop*, 77.
72 Tanahashi, *Moon in a Dewdrop*, 70.
73 William Faulkner, *Requiem for a Nun* (New York: Vintage Books, 1975), 80.
74 James Baldwin, *The Price of the Ticket: Collected Nonfiction: 1948–1985* (Boston: Beacon Press, 2021), 414.
75 Tanahashi, *Moon in a Dewdrop*, 80.
76 Cleary, *Flower Ornament Scripture*, 751.
77 Jennifer Browdy de Hernandez, *Women Writing Resistance: Essays on Latin America and the Caribbean* (Cambridge, MA: South End Press, 2003), 117.
78 Mario T. García, ed., *A Dolores Huerta Reader* (Albuquerque: University of New Mexico Press, 2008), 172.
79 hooks, *All About Love*, 159.
80 Hamar, *Reflecting Mirrors*, 302.
81 Connelly, *Vasubandhu's "Three Natures,"* 180.

82 Cleary, *Flower Ornament Scripture*, 1029.
83 McBride, *Collected Works of Korean Buddhism*, 252.
84 Aylesa Forsee, *Albert Einstein: Theoretical Physicist* (New York: Macmillan, 1963), 81.
85 McBride, *Collected Works of Korean Buddhism*, 82.
86 Cook, *Hua-yen Buddhism*, 76.
87 Lorde, *Sister Outsider*, 110.
88 Cleary, *Entry Into the Inconceivable*, 139.
89 Cleary, *Flower Ornament Scripture*, 242.
90 Uchiyama, *Opening the Hand of Thought*, 65.
91 Uchiyama, *Opening the Hand of Thought*, 30.
92 Grant, *Daughters of Emptiness*, 117.
93 Hamar, *Reflecting Mirrors*, 316.
94 Wayman, *Lion's Roar of Queen Śrīmālā*, 92.
95 Cleary, *Entry Into the Realm of Reality*, 392.
96 Cleary, *Flower Ornament Scripture*, 1272.
97 Brunnhölzl, *Compendium of the Mahayana*, 1:209.
98 Bodhi, *In the Buddha's Words*, 365.
99 Cleary, *Flower Ornament Scripture*, 1483.
100 McBride, *Collected Works of Korean Buddhism*, 262.
101 Cleary, *Entry Into the Inconceivable*, 162.
102 Tanahashi, *Moon in a Dewdrop*, 69.
103 Cleary, *Blue Cliff Record*, 477.
104 Chang, *Buddhist Teaching of Totality*, 142.
105 Aitken, *Gateless Barrier*, 120.
106 Cleary, *Entry Into the Inconceivable*, 70.
107 Leighton, *Cultivating the Empty Field*, 90.
108 Connelly, *Inside the Grass Hut*, 65.
109 Cleary, *Entry Into the Inconceivable*, 74.
110 Ben Connelly, "Oneness With Every Stitch," *Tricycle: The Buddhist Review* 27, no. 2 (Winter 2016): 74.
111 Julch, *Middle Kingdom and the Dharma Wheel*, 340.
112 McBride, *Collected Works of Korean Buddhism*, 362.
113 Cleary, *Entry Into the Inconceivable*, 73.
114 Cleary, *Entry Into the Inconceivable*, 74.
115 Cleary, *Flower Ornament Scripture*, 1311.
116 Cleary, *Entry Into the Realm of Reality*, 388.

117 Cleary, *Entry Into the Realm of Reality*, 390.
118 Cleary, *Entry Into the Realm of Reality*, 392.
119 Cleary, *Entry Into the Inconceivable*, 126.
120 McBride, *Collected Works of Korean Buddhism*, 162.
121 Cleary, *Flower Ornament Scripture*, 88.
122 Brunnhölzl, *Compendium of the Mahayana*, 3:1374.
123 McBride, *Collected Works of Korean Buddhism*, 173.
124 Leighton, *Cultivating the Empty Field*, 72.
125 Chang, *Buddhist Teaching of Totality*, 125.
126 Grant, *Daughters of Emptiness*, 43.
127 McBride, *Collected Works of Korean Buddhism*, 285.
128 Hakeda, *Awakening of Faith*, 58.
129 Nearman, *Shōbōgenzō*, 435.
130 Cleary, *Flower Ornament Scripture*, 364.
131 McBride, *Collected Works of Korean Buddhism*, 278.
132 Bodhi, *In the Buddha's Words*, 142.
133 Cleary, *Flower Ornament Scripture*, 1358–59.
134 Cleary, *Entry Into the Realm of Reality*, 108.
135 Dharmamitra, *Flower Adornment Sutra*, 1888–89.
136 Cleary, *Flower Ornament Scripture*, 103.
137 Kimmerer, *Braiding Sweetgrass*, 222.
138 Tanahashi, *Moon in a Dewdrop*, 69.
139 Grant, *Zen Echoes*, 49.
140 Cleary, *Entry Into the Inconceivable*, 45.
141 Cleary, *Flower Ornament Scripture*, 1494.
142 James Baldwin, *No Name in the Street* (New York: Knopf Doubleday, 2013), 55.
143 McBride, *Collected Works of Korean Buddhism*, 303.
144 Hakeda, *Awakening of Faith*, 90.
145 Connelly, *Inside Vasubandhu's Yogacara*, 158.
146 bell hooks, *bell hooks: The Last Interview and Other Conversations* (New York: Melville House, 2023), 33.
147 Caplow and Moon, *Hidden Lamp*, 65.
148 James Baldwin, *The Price of the Ticket: Collected Nonfiction: 1948–1985* (Boston: Beacon Press, 2021), 379.
149 George Yancy and bell hooks, "bell hooks: Buddhism, the Beats and Loving Blackness," *New York Times*, December 10,

2015, https://archive.nytimes.com/opinionator.blogs.nytimes.com/2015/12/10/bell-hooks-buddhism-the-beats-and-loving-blackness/.

150 Connelly, *Inside Vasubandhu's Yogacara.*

151 McBride, *Collected Works of Korean Buddhism*, 291.

152 Busshō Lahn, *Singing and Dancing Are the Voice of the Law: A Commentary on Hakuin's "Song of Zazen"* (Rhinebeck, NY: Monkfish Book Publishing, 2022).

153 Cleary, *Flower Ornament Scripture*, 1148.

154 Caplow and Moon, *Hidden Lamp*, 299.

155 Bodhi, *In the Buddha's Words*, 366.

156 John C. Hammerback and Richard J. Jensen, *The Rhetorical Career of Cesar Chavez* (College Station, TX: Texas A&M University Press, 2003), 117.

157 Martin Luther King Jr., *Strength to Love* (Boston: Beacon Press, 2019), xi.

158 Cleary, *Flower Ornament Scripture*, 64.

159 AN 4.32, *Sangaha Sutta*, https://www.accesstoinsight.org/tipitaka/an/an04/an04.032.than.html.

160 Tanahashi, *Moon in a Dewdrop*, 44.

161 McBride, *Collected Works of Korean Buddhism*, 157.

162 Leighton, *Cultivating the Empty Field*, 72.

163 Easwaran, *Dhammapada*, 151.

164 Grant, *Daughters of Emptiness*, 140.

165 Cleary, *Flower Ornament Scripture*, 1277.

166 Kimmerer, *Braiding Sweetgrass*, 222.

167 Cleary, *Flower Ornament Scripture*, 1223.

168 Chang, *Buddhist Teaching of Totality*, 224.

169 Connelly, *Vasubandhu's "Three Natures."*

170 Cleary, *Entry Into the Inconceivable*, 125.

171 Bodhi, *In the Buddha's Words*, 75.

172 McBride, *Collected Works of Korean Buddhism*, 200.

173 Cleary, *Flower Ornament Scripture*, 1148.

174 Cleary, *Flower Ornament Scripture*, 1006, 1003, 372, respectively.

175 Brunnhölzl, *Compendium of the Mahayana*, 3:1374.

176 Quoted in Karchmer, *Seeing Red*, 87.

177 Bodhi, *In the Buddha's Words*, 367.

178 Cleary, *Entry Into the Realm of Reality*, 392.

Bibliography

Aitken, Robert. *Gateless Barrier: The Wu-Men Kuan (Mumonkan)*. New York: North Point Press, 1991.

Bodhi, Bhikkhu. *In the Buddha's Words: An Anthology of Discourses from the Pali Canon*. Boston: Wisdom Publications, 2005.

Brunnhölzl, Karl. *A Compendium of the Mahāyāna: Asanga's Mahāyānasaṃgraha and Its Indian and Tibetan Commentaries*. Boulder, CO: Snow Lion, 2018.

Caplow, Florence, and Susan Moon. *The Hidden Lamp: Stories from Twenty-Five Centuries of Awakened Women*. Somerville, MA: Wisdom Publications, 2013.

Chang, Garma C. C. *The Buddhist Teaching of Totality: The Philosophy of Hwa Yen Buddhism*. University Park: Pennsylvania State University Press, 1971.

Cheng Chien Bhikshu. *Manifestation of the Tathāgata: Buddhahood According to the Avataṃsaka Sūtra*. Boston: Wisdom Publications, 1993.

Cleary, Thomas. *Entry Into the Inconceivable: An Introduction to Hua-yen Buddhism*. Honolulu: University of Hawaii Press, 1983.

———. *Entry Into the Realm of Reality*. Boston: Shambhala Publications, 1987.

———. *The Flower Ornament Scripture: A Translation of the Avatamsaka Sutra*. Boston: Shambhala Publications, 1993.

Cleary, Thomas and J. C. Cleary. *The Blue Cliff Record*. Boston: Shambhala Publications, 1977.

Connelly, Ben. *Inside the Grass Hut: Living Shitou's Classic Zen Poem*. Somerville, MA: Wisdom Publications, 2014.

———. *Inside Vasubandhu's Yogacara: A Practitioner's Guide*. Somerville, MA: Wisdom Publications, 2016.

———. *Vasubandhu's "Three Natures": A Practitioner's Guide for Liberation*. Somerville, MA: Wisdom Publications, 2022.

Cook, Francis H. *Hua-yen Buddhism: The Jewel Net of Indra*. University Park: Pennsylvania State University Press, 1977.

Daehaeng. *No River to Cross: Trusting the Enlightenment that's Always Right Here*. Somerville, MA: Wisdom Publications, 2007.

Dharmamitra, Bhikshu. *The Flower Adornment Sutra*. Seattle: Kalavinka Press, 2022.

Easwaran, Eknath, trans. *The Dhammapada*. Tomales, CA: Nilgiri Press, 2007.

Ferguson, Andy. *Zen's Chinese Heritage: The Masters and Their Teachings*. Somerville, MA: Wisdom Publications, 2011.

Garfield, James. *The Fundamental Wisdom of the Middle Way: Nāgārjuna's Mūlamadhyamakakārikā*. Oxford, England: Oxford University Press, 1995.

Gimello, Robert M., and Peter Gregory, eds. *Studies in Ch'an and Huayan*. Honolulu: University of Hawaii Press, 1983.

Gimello, Robert. *Chih-Yeh and the Foundations of Hua-Yen Buddhism*. PhD diss., Columbia University, 1976.

Grant, Beata. *Daughters of Emptiness: Poems of Chinese Buddhist Nuns*. Somerville, MA: Wisdom Publications, 2003.

———. *Zen Echoes: Classic Koans with Verse Commentaries by Three Female Zen Masters*. Somerville, MA: Wisdom Publications, 2017.

Gregory, Peter N. *Tsung-Mi and the Sinification of Buddhism*, Honolulu: University of Hawaii Press, 2002.

Hakeda, Yoshito S. *The Awakening of Faith: Attributed to Aśvaghosha*. New York: Columbia University Press, 2006.

Hamar, Imre, ed. *Reflecting Mirrors: Perspectives on Huayan Buddhism*. Wiesbaden, Germany: Harrassowitz Verlag, 2007.

Hanh, Thich Nhat. *Buddha Mind, Buddha Body: Walking Toward Enlightenment*. Berkeley, CA: Parallax, 2007.

———. *Understanding Our Mind*. Berkeley, CA: Parallax, 2006.

hooks, bell. *Ain't I a Woman?* New York: Routledge, 1981.

———. *All About Love: New Visions*. New York: Harper Perennial, 2000.

Hsüan Hua, trans. and commentary. *Śūraṅgama Sūtra: A New Translation*. Ukiah, CA: Buddhist Text Translation Society, 2017.

Julch, Thomas. *The Middle Kingdom and the Dharma Wheel: Aspects of the Relationship Between the Buddhist Saṃgha and the State in Chinese History*. Boston: Brill, 2016.

Kachru, Sonam. *Other Lives: Mind and World in Indian Buddhism*. New York: Columbia University Press, 2021.

Keel, Hee Sung. *Chinul: The Founder of the Korean Sŏn Tradition*. Berkeley, CA: University of California at Berkeley, 1984.

Kimmerer, Robin Wall. *Braiding Sweetgrass: Indigenous Wisdom, Scientific Knowledge, and the Teachings of Plants*. Minneapolis, MN: Milkweed Editions, 2015.

Leighton, Taigen Dan. *Cultivating the Empty Field: The Silent Illumination of Zen Master Hongzhi*. Boston: Tuttle Publishing, 2000.

Lorde, Audre. *Sister Outsider: Essays and Speeches*. Berkeley, CA: Crossing Press, 2007.

McBride, Richard D., ed. *Collected Works of Korean Buddhism*, Volume 4. Seoul, South Korea: Jogye Order of Korean Buddhism, 2012.

McBride, Richard D. "Dharani and Mantra in Contemporary Korean Buddhism: A Textual Ethnography of Spell Materials for Popular Consumption," *Journal of the International Association of Buddhist Studies* 42 (2019): 361–403.

Ming-Wood, Liu. "The P'an-Chiao System of the Hua-Yen School in Chinese Buddhism," *Toung Pao* 67 (1981), no. 1–2: 28.

Murcott, Susan. *The First Buddhist Women: Poems and Stories of Awakening*. Berkeley, CA: Parallax Press, 1991.

Mu Soeng. *Thousand Peaks: Korean Zen—Tradition & Teachers*. Cumberland, RI: Primary Point Press, 1991.

Ñāṇamoli, Bhikkhu, and Bhikkhu Bodhi. *The Middle Length Discourses of the Buddha: A Translation of the Majjhima Nikāya*. Somerville, MA: Wisdom Publications, 2009.

Nearman, Hubert, trans. *Shōbōgenzō: The Treasure House of the Eye of the True Teaching*. Mount Shasta, CA: Shasta Abbey Press, 2007.

Odin, Steve. *Process Metaphysics and Hua-Yen Buddhism*. New York: State University of New York Press, 1982.

Park, Jin Y. *Buddhism and Postmodernity: Zen, Huayan, and the Possibility of Postmodern Ethics*. Lanham, MD: Lexington Books, 2008.

Pine, Red, trans. *The Lankavatara Sutra: Translation and Commentary*. Berkeley, CA: Counterpoint, 2012.

Powers, John, trans. *Wisdom of Buddha: The Saṁdhinirmocana Mahāyāna Sūtra*. Berkeley, CA: Dharma Publishing, 1995.

Tanahashi, Kazuaki, ed. *Moon in a Dewdrop: Writings of Zen Master Dōgen*. New York: North Point Press, 1985.

Thurman, Robert, trans. *The Holy Teaching of Vimalakīrti: A Mahāyāna Scripture.* University Park: Pennsylvania State University Press, 1976.

Uchiyama, Kosho. *Opening the Hand of Thought: Foundations of Zen Buddhist Practice*. Somerville, MA: Wisdom Publications, 2004.

Wayman, Alex, and Hideko Wayman, trans. *The Lion's Roar of Queen Śrīmālā: A Buddhist Scripture on the Tathāgatagarbha Theory*. Buddhist Tradition Series 10. Delhi: Motilal Banarsidass, 1990. First published 1974 by Columbia University Press (New York).

Wright, Dale S. "The 'Thought of Enlightenment' in Fa-tsang's Hua-yen Buddhism." *The Eastern Buddhist*, n.s., 33, no. 2 (2001): 99.

Index

About the Author and Translator

Ben Connelly is a Soto Zen teacher and Dharma heir in the Katagiri lineage. He also teaches mindfulness in a wide variety of secular contexts including police training and addiction recovery groups. He works with multi-faith groups focused on intersectional liberation, racial justice, and climate justice. Ben serves the Minnesota Zen Meditation Center, travels to teach across the United States, has written for *Tricycle* and *Lion's Roar* magazines, and is author of *Inside the Grass Hut, Inside Vasubandhu's Yogacara, Mindfulness and Intimacy,* and *Vasubandhu's "Three Natures."*

Weijen Teng is chair of the Department of Buddhist Studies at Dharma Drum Institute of Liberal Arts, Taiwan. He completed his BA degree in Pali and Theravada Buddhism at the University of Kelaniya, Sri Lanka, and his MA in Sanskrit at the University of Poona, India. He enrolled in an MA program in Religious Studies at the University of

Chicago and received his PhD in Religious Studies at Harvard University. Dr. Teng's research interests include the Buddhist theory of mind and meditation, the intellectual history of Chinese Buddhism, and more recently, Buddhism and modernity.

What to Read Next from Wisdom Publications

Vasubandhu's "Three Natures"
A Practitioner's Guide for Liberation
Ben Connelly

"This book is an inspiring model of the new face of Buddhism; it opens many doors to personal and social transformation, sorely needed. This is a wonderful read that made both my heart and mind sing with fresh, meaningful possibilities."—Dr. Larry Ward, author of *America's Racial Karma: An Invitation to Heal*

Inside Vasubandhu's Yogacara
A Practitioner's Guide
Ben Connelly

"Through Connelly's luminous teaching, some of Yogacara's most vivid and inspiring innovations come to life.... Newcomers and adherents to this lesser-known Buddhist school alike are lucky to have Connelly as an exceptional guide to the central themes of Yogacara."—*Publishers Weekly* Starred Review

Inside the Grass Hut
Living Shitou's Classic Zen Poem
Ben Connelly

Enter the mind and practice of Zen: apply the insights of one of Zen's classic poems to your life—here and now.

Mindfulness and Intimacy
Ben Connelly

Mindfulness is an ancient and powerful practice of awareness and nonjudgmental discernment that can help us ground ourselves in the present moment, with the world and our lives just as they are.

Footprints on the Journey
One Year Following the Path of Dzogchen Master Khenpo Sodargye
Khenpo Sodargye

Inspiring diary entries from a challenging year in the life of renowned Dzogchen master Khenpo Sodargye demonstrate right conduct on the path to liberation.

MIND SKY
Zen Teaching on Living and Dying
Jakusho Kwong

"This is a wise and beautiful book of heart teachings by a great Soto Zen teacher, Jakusho Kwong-roshi, who shows the way to open infinite Dharma doors through Zen practice."—Roshi Joan Halifax, abbot, Upaya Zen Center, author of *Standing at the Edge* and *Being with Dying*

About Wisdom Publications

Wisdom Publications is the leading publisher of classic and contemporary Buddhist books and practical works on mindfulness. To learn more about us or to explore our other books, please visit our website at wisdom.org or contact us at the address below.

Wisdom Publications
132 Perry Street
New York, NY 10014 USA

We are a 501(c)(3) organization, and donations in support of our mission are tax deductible.

Wisdom Publications is affiliated with the Foundation for the Preservation of the Mahayana Tradition (FPMT).